CLINICAL IMPLICATIONS OF THE FAMILY LIFE CYCLE

James C. Hansen, Editor
Howard A. Liddle, Volume Editor

The Family Therapy Collections

AN ASPEN PUBLICATION ®

Aspen Systems Corporation
Rockville, Maryland
Royal Tunbridge Wells
1983

Library of Congress Cataloging in Publication Data
Main entry under title:

Clinical implications of the family life cycle.

(The Family therapy collections, ISSN 0735-9152; 7)
Includes bibliographies.
1. Family psychotherapy. 2. Family. I. Hansen,
James C. II. Liddle, Howard A. III. Series. [DNLM:
1. Family. 2. Family therapy.
WM 430.5.F2 C6415] RC488.5.C59   1983
616.89'156   83-9238
ISBN 0-89443-607-4

Publisher: John Marozsan
Managing Editor: Margot Raphael
Editorial Services: Ruth Judy
Printing and Manufacturing: Debbie Collins

The Family Therapy Collections series is indexed in
Psychological Abstracts and the PsycINFO database.

Library of Congress Catalog Card Number: 83-9238
ISBN:0-89443-607-4
ISSN: 0735-9152

Printed in the United States of America

1 2 3 4 5

To the memory of
Edward L. Flemming
mentor, friend, and
systems thinker extraordinaire
H.A.L.

Table of Contents

Board of Editors

ix

Contributors

Volume Editor
HOWARD A. LIDDLE

W. ROBERT BEAVERS
University of Texas Health Science
Center
Southwest Family Institute
Dallas, Texas

DOUGLAS C. BREUNLIN
Institute for Juvenile Reseach
Chicago, Illinois

LEE COMBRINCK-GRAHAM
Hahnemann University
Philadelphia, Pennsylvania

GEORGE DOUB
Eastfield Children's Center
Campbell, California

DAVID KANTOR
Kantor Family Institute
The Family Center
Cambridge, Massachusetts

VIRGINIA MORGAN MCFADDEN
Eastfield Children's Center
Campbell, California

GEORGE W. SABA
Midwest Family Resource
Associates
Chicago, Illinois

MICHAEL I. VICKERS
Kantor Family Institute
Divorce Resource and Mediation
Center
Cambridge, Massachusetts

FROMA WALSH
University of Chicago
Northwestern University Medical
School
Chicago, Illinois

MARY F. WHITESIDE
Ann Arbor Center for the Family
Ann Arbor, Michigan

DONALD S. WILLIAMSON
Houston Family Institute
Houston, Texas

Preface

The Family Therapy Collections is a quarterly publication in which topics of current and specific interest to family therapists are reviewed. Each volume serves as a source of information for the practicing professional by translating theory and research into practical applications. The articles, authored by practicing professionals, provide in-depth coverage of a single aspect of family therapy.

This volume focuses on the clinical implications of the family life cycle, the stages through which a family moves. It emphasizes the development of a family, including intergenerational transmission and the developmental sequences in nuclear families, i.e., marrying, raising young children, parenting adolescents, launching children, and adjusting to an empty nest. Families may experience difficulties around transition points in the cycle, and not all families follow a "normal" cycle. Sometimes disruptions in the family life cycle produce symptoms and dysfunctional behaviors. In this volume, therapists are given information about various aspects of life cycles, as well as appropriate interventions.

The editor of this volume is Howard A. Liddle, Ed.D. Dr. Liddle is currently the director of the Behavioral Sciences Program, Division of Family and Community Medicine, University of California School of Medicine, San Francisco and is on the faculty of the Mental Research Institute, Palo Alto, California. He is the former director of the Family Systems Program, Institute for Juvenile Research in Chicago. Dr. Liddle has taught family therapy at several institutions over the past 10 years, including the University of Illinois Medical School, Northwestern University, Temple University, the Eastern Pennsylvania Psychiatric Institute, the Illinois School of Professional Psychology, and Northern Illinois University. Other postdoctorate experience includes 2 years of training at the Philadelphia Child Guidance Clinic.

Dr. Liddle has published widely in the field of family therapy, including a book with George Saba titled *Family Therapy Training and Supervision: Creating Contexts of Competence*. In addition, he serves on the editorial board of three family therapy journals. He is a charter member of the American Family Therapy Association, a fellow in the American Orthopsychiatric Association, an Approved Supervisor in the American Association for Marriage and Family Therapy, and a member of the American Psychological Association.

James C. Hansen
Editor
September, 1983

Introduction

Although prevalent in the theoretical and research literature of family studies/family sociology for some time, the family life cycle paradigm has only recently achieved widespread emphasis in the family therapy field. We are, therefore, at a formative and exploratory phase in the conceptual and clinical incorporation of the family life cycle as a potentially useful framework. This volume aims at investigating some of the theoretic and therapeutic possibilities of the family life cycle in family therapy, as well as an articulation of this emerging concept's limitations, given its present stage of formulation.

As a point of departure, Douglas Breunlin, director of the Family Systems Program of the Institute for Juvenile Research in Chicago, presents a four-stage model of family therapy, designed specifically to help families successfully negotiate their life cycle transitions. His paper creatively demonstrates the interdependence and coherence of a family life cycle paradigm with a therapeutic model of change.

In extending his earlier theoretic formulations about family functioning, David Kantor, director of the Kantor Family Institute in Cambridge, Massachusetts, offers a complex yet rich developmentally grounded therapeutic model. Kantor's approach encompasses a variety of levels and perspectives—individual, spousal/parental, familial—and uses this multicontext appreciation to suggest appropriate focus and interventions during the stages of therapy.

Lee Combrinck-Graham, director of the Marital and Family Therapy Program of Hahnemann Medical College in Philadelphia, details clearly the fine movements of families with young children, and how these family structures necessarily shift as the children enter school age. Her descriptive mastery in defining the changing process issues during this intimate stage of development provides therapists with the invaluable insights of an expert observer of family life.

W. Robert Beavers, director of the Southwestern Family Institute in Dallas, presents an eminently practical compendium of suggestions for individuals and couples struggling to redefine relationships with their families of origin. He offers appealing alternatives for marital partners to help each other with the overzealous and overambitious "missionary" stance often taken in relation to one's parents.

Expanding upon his growing body of impressive work in this area, Donald Williamson of the Houston Family Institute details his family life cycle premises and basic design of a consultation model designed to foster personal development in adults. He further orients therapists to the special clinical problems that arise when adults renegotiate the "intergenerational politics" of family of origin relationships.

In his second contribution to this volume, David Kantor teams with Michael Vickers, a faculty member at the Kantor Family Institute and director of Divorce Mediation Associates in Cambridge, to offer a description of the process of divorce at different stages of the family life cycle. Through the presentation of diverse case material, these authors demonstrate how diverse familial interactional patterns can be translated into specific therapist goals and positive clinical outcome.

A multifaceted examination of remarriage from a family life cycle perspective is the subject of the article by Mary Whiteside, clinical psychologist with the Ann Arbor Center for Family Research and Training. Whiteside deftly describes the manner in which, as she puts it, many life cycle threads must be interwoven in the fabric of remarried families at different stages of their development.

Froma Walsh's article addresses one of the inevitable occurrences in all families' lives—the manner in which death and loss affect a family's life cycle issues. Walsh manages to accurately portray the process issues of this universally difficult aspect of family life, as well as offering pragmatic clinical assessment and intervention ideas for the therapist facing these stressful situations.

Virginia McFadden and George Doub of the Eastfield Children's Center in Campbell, California describe their work in the often-neglected area of applying family systems/therapy principles in a preventive context—teaching families about effective ways of coping with inevitable life cycle difficulties. Their model program, at another level, challenges therapists to reconsider the traditional clinical definition of their roles.

The closing article, by George Saba, director of training at Midwest Family Resource Associates in Chicago and myself, examines the difficulties inherent in clinical application of the family life cycle, especially in light of its current degree and nature of formulation. Additionally, we offer proactive guidelines for further conceptual refinement, and assessment and intervention-generation potential of the family life cycle in clinical practice.

In conclusion, the following articles offer much theoretical diversity and practical relevance. This volume is intended both as an advancement of our knowledge of the family life cycle as it can be applied to the practice of family therapy, and as a stimulus for therapists' efforts to develop a personal, evolving model of therapy. It is hoped that these contributions will assist therapists in exploring the specific implications of the family life cycle in their own everyday clinical work. In this regard, volumes such as this can only sketch aspects of some of the issues involved—the difficult clinical decisions about the relevance and application of this or any paradigm remain with the individual therapist—and perhaps this is as it should and must be.

Howard A. Liddle
Volume Editor
September, 1983

1. Therapy in Stages: A Life Cycle View

Douglas C. Breunlin, MSSA
Director
Family Systems Program
Institute for Juvenile Research
Chicago, Illinois

SINCE ITS FIRST APPEARANCE IN THE LITERATURE (Haley, 1973; Solomon, 1973), the family life cycle paradigm has had a major impact on the way family therapists conceptualize family functioning. In the past, it was believed that problems arose as a result of family psychopathology. With the family life cycle approach, a problem is viewed as a developmental impasse, arising when a family is negotiating a transition from one stage of the life cycle to the next. Correspondingly, therapy is no longer focused on curing psychopathology, but on resolving a particular developmental impasse. This life cycle view not only has contributed to the optimism with which most family therapists view the potential for problem resolution, but also has influenced the choice of treatment strategies.

Once it was recognized that most family problems are linked to life cycle transitions, therapists tried to understand the nature of the transition process. Realizing that a transition necessitates a fundamental shift in how a family operates (in terms of structure, rules, and interaction), Hughes, Berger, and Wright (1978) connected the concept of a transition to that of second order change (Watzlawick, Weakland, & Fisch, 1974), that is, one that alters the rules governing the family's interaction. This connection has greatly influenced contemporary thinking about the transition process, because the nature of a second order change involves discontinuity. In other words, for a family to make a successful transition from one stage of the life cycle to another, it must experience a discontinuous process of change in family organization (Hoffman, 1980; Weeks & Wright, 1979). Discontinuous changes are irreversible; once a family makes a leap to a new organization, it cannot return to the previous organization.

The clinical implications of this life cycle model are considerable, because conceptually the therapist is organized to plan the therapy in such a way as to produce a second order change through a discontinuous leap. Not surprisingly, much of the literature concerning therapy based on this model places a heavy emphasis on the use of paradoxical strategies (such as symptom or system prescription) as the preferred intervention for producing the discontinuous leap (Hoffman, 1980, 1981; Hughes et al., 1978). The net result is an elegant theory on which are based sophisticated interventions that frequently produce dramatic outcomes. This approach, however, poses difficulties for therapists who do not view change as discontinuous and who choose not to work in an exclusively paradoxical way (Breunlin, 1982; Falicov, Schnitman, Breunlin, Sluzki, Hoffman, & McGoldrick, 1981). An alternative model of the transition process, one involving stages rather than discontinuity, can be constructed from the work of Haley (1973, 1976,

1981), who introduced the concepts of the life cycle and therapy in stages into the family therapy literature.

THE LIFE CYCLE MODEL

In his original presentation of the life cycle, Haley (1973) did not elaborate on the nature of the transition process other than to state that "symptoms appear when there is a disruption in the unfolding life cycle of a family" (p. 42). He argued further that the symptom is "a signal that a family has difficulty getting past a stage of the life cycle" (p. 42). Hence, the nature of a failed transition lies more in the failure to complete a process rather than failure to initiate it. Haley (1973) used the therapeutic wizardry of Milton Erickson to illustrate how a therapist can assist a family in completing the transition process; although the vignettes he presented are entertaining and brilliant, it is difficult to distill from them therapeutic principles to guide the average therapist.

It was not until 1976, when Haley's *Problem Solving Therapy* was published, that general principles began to emerge; even then, however, they were not clearly linked to a model of the life cycle. While accepting a developmental view of symptoms, Haley focused primarily on the presentation of a model of therapy geared to solve problems. Haley did not refute the notion of a discontinuous leap, but his model of therapy suggests that change is more gradual and occurs in stages; consequently, a therapist should organize therapy in stages. The key to a stage-based therapy is the recognition that, having developed an abnormal way of functioning, a family with a problem cannot move in one stage to function normally. Rather, to resolve the problem the therapist must create one or more intermediate stages that, although abnormal, move the family closer to normal function.

Haley (1976) used the classic example of a family that deals with a symptomatic child by having one parent become overinvolved while the other is peripheral. This abnormal situation may be approached in several ways. One is to create another abnormal situation in which the peripheral parent is placed in charge of the child and the overinvolved parent disengaged. This intermediate stage prepares the way for the next stage, i.e., the marital disharmony that emerges when the overinvolved parent's access to the child is blocked. This allows the therapist to shift attention from the symptoms of the child to the difficulties in the marriage. As these difficulties are resolved, the family enters its final, normal stage in which the family functions normally and the therapist disengages. Although Haley was not explicit about the connection in *Problem Solving Therapy*, it is possible to link his concept of therapy in stages with the life cycle by noting that problems result from difficulties that families experience in making a transition. Hence, just as therapy based on stages is recommended to solve problems, it is applicable to the problem of a failed transition.

With the publication of *Leaving Home* (1980), Haley made clear links between the life cycle model and therapy in stages. In this work, for example, he stated that a young adult's failure to move away from home indicates that the family is failing to complete the leaving home process. Therapy is organized to circumvent the protective function of the young adult's position in the family, assist the young adult to leave home, and hence complete the life cycle transition. Once again, Haley proposed a model of therapy based on clearly defined stages, this time proposing four stages:

1. getting the young adult out of an institution such as a hospital and into a family setting
2. putting the parents in charge of the young adult
3. dealing with apathy and/or trouble making
4. disengaging

In this therapy model, the second stage may be viewed as abnormal because the parents treat the young adult as a child. The third stage parallels the shift to marital disharmony in the model discussed earlier, because it deals with the consequences of change precipitated by an organizational unbalancing accomplished in the abnormal stage.

By combining the concepts regarding therapy in stages presented in *Problem Solving Therapy* and *Leaving Home,* it is possible to define the therapy stages essential to help a family complete a transition: (1) engage the family, (2) establish an abnormal stage to unbalance the family, (3) deal with the consequences of change, and (4) normalize family functioning and disengage from therapy. In the actual process of therapy, the stages may overlap, and to some extent the punctuation essential to describe the therapy is arbitrary.

Engaging the Family

There are equivalents in the other treatment models (Minuchin, 1974; Haley, 1976) for the stages in which the family is engaged, as this is essential to ensure the continuity of therapy. In some cases, engaging the family may require only part of the initial session; in other, more complex and difficult cases, it may take several sessions. An important component of the work done during this stage is laying the groundwork for the unbalancing stage. The therapeutic system must be well established, and the family members who will participate in the unbalancing must be well prepared. The larger context must also be readied; otherwise, other institutions (e.g., schools or hospitals) may undermine the therapy by blocking the unbalancing maneuvers or by mishandling the consequences triggered by the unbalancing.

In this stage, the therapist should frame the problem in life cycle or developmental terms so that the goals of therapy include not only the resolution of the immediate problem, but also the completion of a transition. When the failed transition is readily apparent (e.g., going to school or leaving home), the therapist should talk openly about completing it as one of the goals of therapy. The failed transition may not be readily apparent, however, sometimes because the family has struggled with it for several years, sometimes because there is not one but a series of failed transitions. In such cases, the symptomatic behavior of a family member may be framed in developmental terms by calling attention to ways in which it is not age-appropriate. For instance, when a 7-year-old screams at a parent, the screaming can be defined as a temper tantrum, which is not age-appropriate. The message to be conveyed is that problem behavior does not indicate madness or badness, but rather a failure to act one's age. Consequently, the goal of therapy is to organize the family to expect and obtain age-appropriate behavior. Once family members accept a life cycle or developmental hypothesis, their readiness to see themselves as instrumental in solving the problem is increased, and the stage is set for unbalancing operations.

Unbalancing the Family

A family unable to make the transition needed at a particular point in its life cycle has evolved a rigid organization that repeatedly attempts to progress developmentally, but without success. Having engaged the family and framed the problem in life cycle or developmental terms, the therapist must help the family attempt a different solution to the impasse. The new solution must be powerful enough to break the impasse; consequently, it is usually abnormal in the sense that the family would not be expected to continue functioning in such a way once the transition is completed. For example, placing two parents in complete charge of an adult offspring is certainly abnormal, but it affords the parents the power they need to insist that their child behave normally.

The unbalancing may be abnormal in another way; it may constitute an ordeal. If a child will not attend school, for example, the peripheral parent, usually the father, may take charge of the child, taking time off work and not infrequently dragging the child physically into the school. The decisiveness of such action and the ordeal it creates for all involved is often sufficient to unbalance the family. The ordeal can be more subtle. In one very religious family, the teen-aged daughter would not attend her freshman year in high school. The parents colluded, being ambivalent about the secular environment the school represented. Using the language of the family, the therapist said that only God could provide a solution and prescribed that the girl sit in her room all day, reading the Bible and awaiting some direction from above. She did so for several days and then found a school that represented a compromise. Younger children can be instructed to do chores or homework all day as a way of creating an ordeal.

The therapist must be careful to prepare the family for the unbalancing intervention and to make it palatable to those who must carry it out. In one case, an adolescent boy had been expelled from school for truancy and fighting; he had been informed that he would not be readmitted to the school's work-study program until he had secured employment. The parents complained that the boy had not found work, but they did not pressure him to take action. He languished at home, doing nothing. The therapist linked the job issue to school and convinced the parents that they must insist the boy look for work. The parents were advised to make certain the boy was out of the house and looking for work the first thing each morning (Haley, 1980). Neither parents nor adolescent were attracted to this solution and accepted it only after very careful and persistent selling and encouragement on the part of the therapist.

Although there is no guarantee that a recommended intervention will be carried out, the chances are increased if all loopholes have been closed. Hence, whatever the solution, all contingencies must be covered and every objection and obstacle overcome. While time-consuming and tedious, this preparatory work is necessary. It is also important to work one step at a time. In the case just cited, for example, the parents expressed concern that the boy would not find a job, in which case their efforts would have been to no avail. The therapist countered by stating that the act of looking was the first step; unless the boy made an effort, nothing would result. It is useful to rehearse the solution in the session, not only to uncover loopholes, but also to convince the family that the recommended solution is feasible.

If the unbalancing intervention has been well designed and carefully implemented, it often produces a change the first time it is applied. In some cases, on the other hand, it must be applied several times before a change is noticed, possibly because the symptomatic individual does not initially believe the abnormal situation will continue. If the symptomatic family member is a child and the parents are initiating the solution, the parents must be prepared to be persistent. To do so requires absolute conviction on the part of both the parents and the therapist. In one family with an encopretic child, the mother was instructed to have nothing to do with the cleanup procedures. The child continued to soil and tried to reengage the mother by smearing feces on his hands and bringing them to the mother until the mother handed them back, stating to the child in no uncertain terms that they belonged to him and he had to be responsible for the cleanup.

The unbalancing stage can be found in many family therapy approaches. In fact, any procedure that unbalances a rigid organization unable to make a transition may be used. If the unbalancing is successful, the impasse will be broken and the family will be able to function in the developmentally appropriate stage of the life cycle. At this point in the therapy the family has changed, but the therapy is not necessarily finished.

Unlike the discontinuous model, the present model takes into account the fact that change has certain consequences, some of which are positive, reinforcing the change, and some of which are negative, undermining the change. Because the discontinuous model includes the concept of irreversibility, therapists who use this model tend not to prolong therapy once change has occurred; those who use the present model, however, include another stage in the therapy to address the consequences of change in an effort to eliminate the possibility of a relapse.

Dealing with the Consequences of Change

In both the Problem Solving and Leaving Home models, Haley (1976, 1980) included stages that anticipate the consequences of change. For example, in the former, marital disharmony can emerge as a consequence of an overinvolved parent's disengagement from a symptomatic child. In the latter, the family may react to the unbalancing stage with apathy or trouble making. The general principle to be applied is that change does not take place without some negative consequences. Failure to address these consequences may undermine the progress achieved through the unbalancing stage and hence render the therapy a failure. In other words, it is not enough to say that the benefit of change will be self-reinforcing or that change itself is permanent because it is irreversible.

Some consequences of change affect the entire family directly, and others affect individual family members (and therefore the entire family indirectly). Negative consequences can produce a recurrence of the problem or the appearance of new problems, and sometimes wrongly convince the therapist that no change has occurred. I do not view these threats as evidence of homeostasis, but rather as signs that with change comes ambivalence which must be addressed if the life cycle transition is to be permanent. Some of the possible consequences of change are regret, anger, fear, and mourning.

When family members are suddenly released from a rigid pattern of interaction and enabled to behave differently, they may regret the time spent in fruitless attempts to make a transition. They often wonder why the strategy that broke the impasse was not attempted earlier. For instance, when a mother's overinvolvement with her children keeps them young, she usually has little time to call her own. When she begins to expect and obtain age-appropriate behavior, she is freed somewhat to think of herself. In such situations, some mothers regret the time needlessly given to their children. The therapist must take care to frame the past benevolently and to usher in the new era gently. The mother's pursuit of her own interests can also produce negative consequences for other relationships; the father, for example, may feel threatened by the new independence. By predicting difficulties, prescribing caution, or even providing support in a relapse, the therapist can help the family adjust to the new behaviors.

Anger is a consequence similar to regret. Parents who have persisted in a hierarchical reversal can become excessively punitive when the unbalancing stage corrects the hierarchy. They may set excessive punishments for misbehavior. The therapist, in such instances, must be extremely cautious; should the parents' choices be challenged as wrong, the therapist will unwittingly undermine the newly formed hierarchy. Initially, the parents must be allowed to select the punishments. Once the hierarchy is corrected, however, the anger can be reframed and the punishments modified to bring them in line with the behavior itself.

Fear always accompanies change, whether it be fear of intimacy, fear of power, fear of control, or simply fear of the unknown. In the classic example in *Problem Solving Therapy*, "A Modern Little Hans" (Haley, 1976), the therapist experienced considerable difficulty in helping the family to resolve marital problems once the abnormal stage had dislodged the symptoms by placing the peripheral father in charge of the presenting problem, the boy's dog phobia. The overinvolvement of mother and son (stated metaphorically by the dog phobia, which prevented the boy from playing outside and generated excessive concern on the part of the mother) and distance of father had begun when the boy was born. The couple had handled the transition to parenthood with the mother becoming overcommitted to the infant and the father having an affair. They had buried the past, but not forgotten it; as the therapist probed the marriage, both spouses resisted, fearing the bitterness and rejection that had never been expressed. The therapist initiated the next stage by reframing the past and giving a directive (husband to choose some way to surprise his wife) that enabled the couple to take a tentative but significant step toward overcoming their fears.

Any life cycle model should take into account the sadness that inevitably marks the passing of a stage in the life of a family. Some form of mourning is normal when the last child is born, goes to school, or leaves home. This mourning, however, can appear as depression or lack of enthusiasm for the changes taking place. One possible response is to remove the reason for mourning, which, in the case of the life cycle, would be to undo the transition. The therapy must frame the mourning as normal and provide opportunities to mourn in a way that does not undermine change.

The stage in which the consequences of change are addressed may actually consist of a series of substages. At this stage, the family is held in position while the change produced by the unbalancing is sealed. When the therapist observes consistency in the family's ability to function in the appropriate stage of the life cycle, it is time to shift to the final stage of normalizing function and disengaging.

Normalizing Family Function and Disengaging from Therapy

When a life cycle model is used to organize family therapy, the preferred outcome is defined in terms of functioning within the appropriate stage of the family life cycle. In this sense, the concept of permanent cure is incompatible with a life cycle model, because it is impossible to guarantee that a family will experience no problems when it encounters another transition.

Normal functioning within an appropriate stage is not easily defined. Haley (1980), for instance, argued that therapy for young adults should be ended when they are symptom-free and engage in activities normal for their age, such as going to school or working. He advised against attempts to socialize young adults further through therapy, arguing that such efforts have a labeling effect. Likewise, Haley did not recommend marital therapy unless the couple specifically requests it; even then he believed it should be undertaken only after their children have begun to function normally. The distinction is between symptom-free and optimal functioning.

Many therapists prolong therapy because they include stages designed to effect optimal functioning. This type of help is warranted when it is requested by the family. When it is not, it is preferable for the therapist to take the view that a successfully completed transition offers new potential for the identified patient and all other family members. This potential is best realized in the natural context of the family.

In normalizing family functioning, the therapist should convey approval to the family for a job well done. This requires skill in framing behavior in a positive way while blocking any negative feelings the family may still have. For instance, when a mother begins to care for an infant properly, the infant's improved health can be emphasized; any criticism of her dealings with the infant is avoided while she gains confidence. In cases involving serious problems, it may be difficult to normalize functioning. Sometimes, it is wise to continue seeing the family or patient on an infrequent basis, but caution must be exercised not to label either as defective.

If the therapist successfully normalizes family functioning, the task of disengaging is comparatively easy—the family agrees, explicitly or implicitly, to handle its own business. Because the consequences of change are not completely predictable, the disengagement should include mechanisms for the family and therapist to recontact one another. The therapist can act as a readily available safety valve.

CONCLUSION

The model of therapy that has been presented is designed to assist families who experience difficulties in making transitions in their life cycle. Based on a view that change is continuous, this approach enables therapy to be a systematic endeavor. The therapist can, to some extent, predict what will happen. In addition, the course of therapy can be evaluated; progress and setbacks fit into a framework, mitigating unrealistic expectations or unwarranted pessimism.

REFERENCES

Breunlin, D.C. *Clinical dimensions of the family life cycle*. Paper presented at the annual conference of the American Association for Marriage and Family Therapy, Dallas, October 1982.

Falicov, C., Schnitman, D., Breunlin, D.C., Sluzki, C., Hoffman, L., & McGoldrick, M. *The family life cycle*. Paper presented at the annual conference of the American Orthopsychiatric Association, New York, 1981.

Haley, J. *Uncommon therapy: The psychiatric techniques of Milton Erickson*. New York: Norton, 1973.

Haley, J. *Problem solving therapy*. New York: Harper Colophon, 1976.

Haley, J. *Leaving home*. New York: McGraw-Hill, 1980.

Hoffman, L. The family life cycle and discontinuous change. In E. Carter & M. McGoldrick (Eds.), *The family life cycle: A framework for family therapy*. New York: Gardner Press, 1980.

Hoffman, L. *Foundations of family therapy: A conceptual framework for systems change*. New York: Basic Books, 1981.

Hughes, S.F., Berger, M., & Wright, L. The family life cycle and clinical intervention. *Journal of Marriage and Family Counseling*, 1978, *4*, 33-39.

Minuchin, S. *Families and family therapy*. Cambridge, MA: Harvard University Press, 1974.

Solomon, M. A developmental conceptual premise for family therapy. *Family Process*, 1973, *12*, 179-188.

Watzlawick, P., Weakland, J., & Fisch, R. *Change: Principles of problem formation and problem resolution*. New York: Norton, 1974.

Weeks, G.R., & Wright, L. Dialectics of the family life cycle. *American Journal of Family Therapy*, 1979, *7*, 85-91.

2. The Structural-Analytic Approach to the Treatment of Family Developmental Crisis

David Kantor, PhD
Director
Kantor Family Institute

Clinical Director
The Family Center
Cambridge, Massachusetts

Since HALEY (1973) FIRST CALLED ATTENTION TO THE RELATIONSHIP between families' problems and their developmental or life cycle stages, this subject has attracted increasingly sophisticated attention from theorists and therapists (Carter & McGoldrick, 1980). Despite Haley, it still seemed that trying to determine how families arrived at a particular state at a particular moment in time was antithetical to systems thinking, with its ahistorical bias and its here-and-now emphasis. Nevertheless, I proceeded to launch two studies.

The first was a case study of one family, a young couple in which the woman was in the 5th month of her first pregnancy. In this study, I followed the woman and her husband over a 4-year period (through audio and video taping, periodic interview, and observation in the home) through three pregnancies and births, and an eventual separation and divorce. This effort led to the concept of critical identity image, which can be viewed as a conceptual link between individual, couple, and family development and can be considered the basis for any clinical activity that utilizes developmental or life stage issues (Kantor, 1977, 1979, 1980).

The second study was a clinical survey in which 20 family therapists interviewed one family each, the total sample representing a broad range of ages, family constructions, types of problems, and life cycle stages. The result of this effort suggested that many, although not all, problems can be best understood as an arrest in the system's development; such an arrest is usually the result of a struggle between two powerful members of the system over who is to have controlling influence over the family's model of reality and, therefore, over its rules and strategies. Furthermore, the best way to ensure that families who are relieved of their problems via therapy actually progress in their development so that problems are less likely to reappear is to address issues of "competing identity claims," which can be seen as the basis for the struggle and developmental derailment.

It can be concluded that the best way to understand family development for the largest number of cases and family types, is not exclusively from the standpoint of "nodal events" (marriage, birth of children, launching of adolescents, and death of partners), but through a consideration of developmental tasks or dilemmas that every intimate system must face, regardless of its construction. This approach is called structural-analytic. It attempts, in a single and still a systems perspective, to accommodate outer and inner, present and past, family and individual systems.

DEVELOPMENT THEORY AND STRUCTURAL ANALYSIS

.Systems development theory will vastly improve our ability to help developmentally derailed families because it shifts the focus from family systems *versus* individuals to family systems *and* individuals *in* systems. Structural analytic theory is a systems development perspective that attempts to further the closing of these unnecessary, clinically disempowering gaps.

Structural analysis takes its name from two sources. It is structural in the sense that all family systems approaches are structural. For example, the targets of change—a boundary (enmeshed, fused), an interpersonal configuration (a negative coalition, a covert alliance, a triangulation), or a pattern (a redundant sequence, a ritual impasse)—can all be viewed as aspects of structures. Further it has been noted that these phenomena occur at "different levels of organization" (Kantor, 1980). Structural analysis is analytic in its conceptual kinship with individual psychodynamic approaches, for example, in its utilization of the past (foundation events located in earlier experiences) and internalizations of past experience that affect current behaviors (critical images, projective identification). The developmental focus of structural-analytic theory is intended to integrate both individual and systems approaches under a single conceptual umbrella in order to describe how systems evolve, experience temporary breakdowns in development, resolve their difficulties, and proceed on their evolutionary course.

IMAGE: THE BASIS OF IDENTITY

Few things are more important than images. Individuals' views of the world, their inner realities, their expectations of others, their ability to share a common language and communicate with others, all result from their inner images. Images are important not only in the quest for individual identity, as they are the contents of identity, but also in the realization of intimate relationships, as they are the foundation of shared reality and thus of a shared identity. In the evolution of a family system for helping family members survive psychologically, socially, and systemically, images are also important. Indeed, they are the very bases for the family model, constituted by the very structures evolved for use in guiding day-to-day actions throughout the family life cycle.

Application: The Rostows

While William Rostow privately struggles with the world's view of him as a notably successful businessman and citizen, he has had no difficulty surviving economically without any public evidence of his inner doubts. Within his family, however, the image of him as a notorious failure both as husband and father is consistently held. Note his daughter Elaine's rude estimate: "My father freaks me out. Everything he does is off the wall. He's a complete jerk." Or his wife Maryanne's prophetic claim: "From the day we married, Bill has failed me whenever I needed him most." Or William Rostow's self-estimate: "Even when I know I'm batting 400, if Maryanne tells me I'm a 200 hitter, I feel and act like a 200 hitter. I hate her for this with a fury, but I can't seem to shake it off."

Images around themes of success and failure, availability and unavailability are William Rostow's contribution to his family's bank of individual and family images and to the family structures that have formed around these images. The family structures in question, which have served to maintain Elaine's symptom formation and problem behavior, take their shape not only from William and his image alone, but also from Maryanne and those of her images that interact systemically with William's to form the disabled structures, periodically resulting in family (as well as individual) developmental crises.

The Rostow family has experienced a series of such developmental breakdowns over the course of its 21-year history. Fourteen-year-old Elaine's seemingly imminent hospitalization, the crisis that brought the family back to therapy (the oldest child, Denise, had been "successfully" treated when she was 17 years old in a family-based therapy that ended 1½ years before), was only the current one. Charles, the middle child, now 17, had had a childhood psychosis, resulting in prolonged psychoanalytic therapy starting when he was 4 years old. Each parent has had psychoanalytic therapy.

Image Defined

An image is defined as an internalized sensory imprint of external events and experiences, usually retained in the form of a memory picture. Images constitute an individual's subjective knowledge structure. They integrate emotion and cognition, sensibility and intellect. Images are emotionally charged structures that may have either positive or negative effects. They persist over time, forming a consistent thread in personality development and integrating a person's identity and development.

Over the course of any therapy, a therapist becomes familiar with a family's image structure through its recurrent themes, explanations of things, and the members' selective responses to the therapist and therapist's environment. In addition, every effective therapist develops ways of using that knowledge of the family's image structure to bring about specific therapeutic change, as anyone must concede who has witnessed the work of such great magicians of therapy as Milton Erickson, Virginia Satir, and Carl Whitaker. The problem for systems therapists is that people have many images, but only a few of these images play crucial parts in their relationship structures. These few, according to structural-analytic theory, are responsible for the identity struggles that derail families developmentally.

Critical Identity Image

Each individual internalizes a special subset of images that concern the self in relation to others. These critical identity images are always actional in nature, involving the self and at least one other person in a describable social context. They are, therefore, images about relationships and relationship structures. An individual's patterned behaviors, his or her characteristic tendencies in relationships, are based on these images.

The Rostows: Maryanne's Critical Image

At age 11, Maryanne Rostow was to be in a school play. Although she was an obviously capable child who had already won her share of honors in the worlds of school and friends, this was in Maryanne's mind a "coming out" of sorts, both for her and her family. It was a ceremony of worth to the world, but more importantly, a testimony of love to (and, as the image shows, from) her parents. Maryanne felt sure of her relationship with her mother, who supported her in whatever she did, especially if her activity involved a demonstration of autonomy (only late in the therapy was it revealed that her mother's habit of rewarding her for her autonomy was experienced as a subtle way of saying, "I can't be bothered to care for you more directly."). She was less sure of her relationship with her father, "a hard working immigrant whose best was never good enough." On the eve of the play's opening, Maryanne set out to make arrangements with her parents for a postperformance celebration. In a manner described as utterly insensitive, her father off-handedly remarked that he would not be able to attend. He could not take the time off from work. Turning to her mother, Maryanne pleaded her cause. Mother merely shrugged. "Do not expect more of men," was her message.

Maryanne fell apart emotionally and physically, but managed to get through the school play. "Still," she said, "I never fully recovered from that disappointment." Burying her feelings, Maryanne continued relations with both her father and her mother in this pattern, her "disappointment" only rarely surfacing. Four years later, with the approach of her graduation, Maryanne again approached her parents with a plan. Again her father declined, and again her mother demurred, but the girl did not retreat: "They have never forgotten the row I created." As a result, her father did attend, however indifferent his commitment and divided his attention. For Maryanne, it was "a victory that left my heart cold."

Events such as these can be called foundation events, as their elements give structure to the image. Foundation events and their elements derive not from single events but from an individual's recurrent experiences, often in quite down-to-earth life contexts. The importance of context in these matters is that it provides the stability of the image's elements, its structure. The importance of the structure of an individual's image is that the image bearer uses it as a basis not only for perceiving and explaining realities, but also for anticipating realities. The importance of reality anticipation in intimate relationships is that the heightened expectancies of one partner, by calling attention to the other's latent tendencies, encourages or even provokes them into becoming manifest. When a wife says to her husband, "I don't wish to behave this way, your constant insinuations *make me* behave this way," she is revealing the power of an image to create its own demons and angels. When each partner's denials of the other's attributions leads to a struggle over whose definitions of reality will prevail, and when they cannot resolve the struggle, the "triangled in" third party is a convenient if not necessary detour.

The Rostows: William's Critical Image

William Rostow is a "disappointment" to Maryanne and has been since the night of their honeymoon. His "unavailability in communication, and especially his unavailability and failure to act strongly on his own initiative as a parent when the kids need him, make intimacy impossible and co-parenting a travesty."

The Rostows came again for therapy for help with their youngest child, Elaine, who manifested "bizarre behaviors" and was "unmanageable." All of Maryanne's waking hours were devoted to Elaine. All of the couple's evening and weekend hours were spent anticipating, fighting over, or dealing with the aftermath of the next crisis. The Rostows were in a massive developmental breakdown, out of which had evolved a set of nearly totally disabled structures for parenting their child.

Together with Elaine, William and Maryanne were involved in an "enmeshed boundary," a "pathological triad," a "disturbed hierarchy."

In its major contribution to the relief of human problems, family therapy has drawn particular attention to the ''perverse triangle.'' The parents, in a conflict they cannot resolve, table their conflict by involving the child, who becomes the third member of the triangle. Quite properly, attention has been on the child, who as symptom bearer of the systemic (i.e., couple) conflict, must be removed from the triangle and, thus, relieved of the symptom or problem behavior. The developmental perspective of structural-analysis draws attention to the couple conflict itself. From this perspective, the basis for the couple conflict is competing (critical identity) images.

Competing Critical Images, Competing Identity Claims

It is every couple's task to evolve a family model or paradigm that explicates the rules and guides family members in construing and dealing with specific aspects of their social environments, both internal and external. The basis for each partner's construction of reality is his or her critical image set. These images not only define reality, but specify how self and other are to behave in the particular contexts that invoke the image. These images then are the sources of family models.

The Image Elicited from William

William: I had been in the basement a long time, writing a long poem. Admittedly a clumsy heartfelt effort, but I tried so hard. It was for Mother, though I never said so. She read it casually and then paused in that condescending way I knew so well. I got the message.

Therapist: Your father?

William: Dad never crossed her. No one does.

Therapist: What exactly did he do?

William: Nothing noticeable. God, maybe that's the point. Anyway, what he did was look at me sadly and drop his eyes to his paper or look away.

William was between 10 and 12 years old when this one of many similarly constructed occurrences took place. Desperate to please his mother, a very gregarious public figure and very successful lawyer, who "to this day confuses performance with love," and a woman who cannot praise

even the highest performance of her three sons because she can always conceive of a better way of doing things. I remember trying "this" out on her, then "that," always with the same result—nothing I did mattered. Whatever expression of myself I offered, it was turned down. The rule was "don't be you, be me." So I began to pretend. I remember retreating deeper and deeper into myself, where, though I was very lonely, I could hate her undetected. How I got back, how I got esteem on my own terms, was to stop showing my real self to her. But what felt to be most crippling was my confusion about my options. On the one hand, she was saying "Do this and you will please me." On the other, she was saying, "You will never succeed in pleasing me." I have never stopped trying.

It is every individual's developmental task to take such negative foundation events and transform them into positive identity claims. Intimate relationships are natural contexts for this transformation process. Most people enter such relationships with incomplete transformations—one source of their intractability in their critical identity image struggles. When they confront one another in identity struggles, they usually present not the image or foundation event, but identity claims, positive assertions of value that derive from the image and its specific elements.

Positive Identity Claims

In his identity struggles with Maryanne, William's claim was: I have an infinite capacity to keep on trying. Why is that not good enough? Maryanne's positive identity claim was: I *know* what is needed in almost any situation. Why can I not depend on you to be sensitive and to act on your own initiative?

Therapy with couples is more difficult when the negative foundation event has not been transformed into a positive identity claim or when the individuals are at very different stages in the transformation process (Kantor, 1979). Maryanne and William had not progressed very far, as can be seen in the queries that they each attached to their claims. Competition over their definitions of reality (and over the rule-supplying family model, rather thoroughly stalled in its development), especially in connection with the assignment and distribution of tasks in raising and caring for their children, had been locked in unresolved struggle for many years. Each child had been caught up in it, Elaine (the primary identified patient) most recently.

Competition over definitions of reality is a natural feature of couple relationships. The structures that come to constitute the family's paradigm are born either of nonconflictual integrations of interacting image elements or from successful resolutions of competing identity claims. A systems development crisis—a temporary breakdown in the rules and mechanisms governing the system—occurs when the couple cannot resolve their identity struggles. In a prolonged breakdown, a disabled structure, i.e., a ritualized sequence of behaviors in which the goals of interaction are systematically unmet, evolves. This, of course, is the infamous redundancy encountered by all family therapists. When these sequences are examined closely, their elements can be shown to result from specific elements in each partner's image.

The Structure of the Image

Critical images are not "just" sensory imprints, internalizations, or (re)constructions of key events. They have a structure of their own that includes three primary elements: (1) a thematic structure, (2) a mood or affect structure, and (3) an action structure. A family's thematic structure—the content of its life, its quality, as manifested in what its members define as important—derives from the interaction of all three image elements in each partner's critical image set. A family's mood or affect structure—its emotional tone (e.g., heavy or light)—itself, also derives from the interaction of all three image elements in each partner's image set. A family's *action structures*, its behavior, and behavior tendencies as manifested in face-to-face relations are similarly derived.

More specifically, a family's action structures are combinations of "*player moves*." There are only four moves or ways people can act in relation to one another. An individual can be (1) a mover, one who defines or initiates an action; (2) a follower, one who agrees with, supports, or continues the action; (3) an opposer, one who challenges or goes against the action; or (4) a bystander, one who witnesses an action, but remains outside, acknowledging neither agreement nor disagreement. A family's action structures consist of specific psychopolitical configurations, and family members tend to combine certain paired moves (e.g., mover-opposer or mover-follower arrangements) in interactions. The character or style of any dyad is known to others from these configurations. Such action structures are partial structures or microstructures. Combinations of microstructures make up the sequences by which a family's pattern structures can be identified.

For therapists, the value of determining the structures of the couple's images is fairly self-evident. Because the Rostows' images were known, it was no surprise to find that Elaine was systemically cultivated as a self-defeating mover who would challengingly disobey her father; that her place in the disturbed hierarchy was safeguarded by the covert coalition she was in with her mother against her father; and that William would fail to initiate or to sustain his own actions because, in this family as in his mother's, he had become a disabled bystander and a covert opposer, discouraged from making strong moves. It also followed that disappointment and confusion as to options, as well as efforts that result not in gratitude but in "a cooling of the heart," were feeling tones that would color the content and texture of the family's life. In retrospect, it even made sense that Maryanne would become ill on her honeymoon; that William would, as she tells it, "clumsily plod on with the motions of sex"; and that thereafter every move on his part as lover and parent would be undermined (she "of the cool heart" finding sustenance for her campaign by her husband's secret rage, forever undetected because of his practiced pattern of token devotions, alternating with a withdrawn unavailability of real self).

There is another, less obvious, value to knowing the couple's image structures. The most interesting and most controversial, issue currently being addressed in the field today deals with the nature of change. Some say that change takes place continuously, in gradual increments, and that the process is governed by principles of homeostasis; some say, discontinuously, in leaps that are unrelated to past or preceding events, the process governed by stochastic principles. Some say both—the process of change is governed by mechanisms associated with the particular paradigm the family is evolving (Kantor & Lehr, 1975).

THE GENESIS OF SYSTEM PATHOLOGY

How do the structural elements of two individual images transpose into a system structure that is, in its essential nature, different from the original structures? The genesis of one Rostow family structure, the perverse triangle, involving Elaine and her two parents, can be used as an example.

Three months after Denise, Elaine's oldest sibling, had been successfully launched from the family and into the world, couple's therapy was begun with Maryanne and William; it enjoyed only modest success, at best. While "communication" improved, the couple could sustain only brief hours of "intimacy," usually just after a session. Sex, however, was nonexistent. (It was learned later that sex had virtually ended on their honeymoon, the children coming as "planned accidents.") It became clear that there was a structural ceiling on what could be accomplished, both because of the depth of the couple's sexual alienation (physical repulsion on Maryanne's part, angry despair on William's) and because Elaine played a key role in her parents' lives.

While Elaine had actually had longstanding problems (according to the most recent neuropsychological examination, "probably related to neuromaturational and psychological factors"), at the time her parents began therapy she had become increasingly defiant of limits and more verbally explosive; was aggressive and uncontrollable at home; was choosing friends who were "acting out" with drugs, sex, and truancy; was attracting attention in the community by bizarre behavior in public places; and began running away from home, asking to be hospitalized or otherwise detained. Therefore, it was agreed to shift the focus to family therapy with Elaine as the identified patient.

The goals in this therapy were to help Denise (the oldest sibling) remain at an appropriate affectional distance from her enmeshing-closed family, to relieve Charles (the middle child) of his responsibility as a parentified child, to detriangulate Elaine from the pathological structure she was in with her parents, and to establish an executive structure capable of delivering both discipline and care for the beleaguered Elaine. In the problem-solving sense, the goal was to keep Elaine from being hospitalized.

Blocking these efforts was the pathological structure in which Maryanne and William would set out to work on their problems, as couple and parents. Elaine would draw attention to herself, in minor ways, at first; Maryanne and William, setting out on separate courses, would undermine each other's efforts. Elaine's provocations would escalate dramatically, requiring strong, often punitive initiatives on William's part. Still covertly undermining each other, the couple would shift the focus of attention from authority and discipline to "Elaine's inherent pathology," a conclusion they shared and one that allowed them to provide care.

In every negative foundation event there is a missing element, a redemptive action that would have made the original experience a positive rather than a negative event. A reexamination of William's image makes this point clear. When William presents his poetic offering to his mother, his father secretly applauds the merits of his son's poem, but fails either to speak up or to buffer against his wife's uncompromising standards. Redemptive moves are missing in the original scenario. Such moves would include a *follower* move, i.e., positive or even some qualified support of the boy's initiative by his mother; an opposer move, i.e., any challenging of his mother's strong position by his father; or, finally, a bystander move, i.e., a neutral position taken by his father, which would serve to bridge mother and son in some way.

In identity struggles these missing image elements are critical. Each partner feels that the missing elements from past structures must be included in the new ones being formed.

In William's ideal model of family, redemptive moves would certainly be present. In turn, that part of Maryanne's ideal family model derived from her competing image would most certainly leave room for others to take initiative and to make strong, caring moves. In the family's characteristic interactions, Maryanne is a terrible follower; a disenchanted, though tirelessly stuck mover; and a ritually stuck opposer. William is a tireless pursuer (a follower of other's strong moves). Having been undone when he made initiating moves in his own family, he became a too-far-removed, and thus a disabled bystander, who covertly opposes the strong moves of others. The dysfunctional structure of which Elaine is an integral part is made up of the following additional elements. Elaine openly opposes her father in a way that neither Maryanne nor William opposed their own powerful and/or inaccessible parents. Seemingly to their own undoing, each parent covertly supports this behavior in their daughter, an admittedly terrible eventuality, but one that can be understood. In an unfortunately perverse sense, Maryanne and William are improving on the models their original families had for making the children in their families feel cared for and competent. Surely, they are trying; clearly, they are not there yet.

Therapy should lead to the establishment of a family model with an improved structure, a structure made complete for each partner by the inclusion of the redemptive element missing from each one's foundation event. The evolution of such ''improved'' structures is every family's goal, and the interaction of elements in the couple's images is the key to the success or failure of these efforts.

TREATMENT CONSIDERATIONS

In therapy based on these ideas, the therapist must: (1) identify accurately ''the couple'' involved in the image struggle; (2) pinpoint the specific developmental task at which the couple is stuck and develop a thorough grasp of the couple's competing images, the elements of these image structures, and the ways in which the image elements affect family structures and other family members; and (3) guide the therapy through the various stages of therapy, each stage with its own goals.

The "Couple"

In this conception, the couple is viewed as the executor of the family's systemic estate. A couple can be any two image-bearing sources of influence, powerful enough to have a triangulating effect on a third party (the triangulated person is not always a child). Any combination of sources is possible—mother and her deceased mother, child and parent, black mother and white society. Some examples of "couples" from my therapy work include

- mother and adolescent son. The triangulated member is the father, whose symptom is episodic rage directed at his wife and disaffection from the son.
- mother and maternal grandmother. The triangulated member is a 6-year-old daughter, whose symptom is fear of abandonment and whose problem is school phobia.
- man and his deceased father. The triangulated member is a wife, who remains in a sexless marriage for 15 years before seeking "individual" therapy.
- a black mother and racist white culture (i.e., "The Man"). The triangulated member is a son, whose symptom is episodic rage directed at the self through drug abuse and at society through self-sacrificial criminal activity, as a result of which he will either be jailed, be killed, or commit suicide.

The image-bearing sources, then, can be living or dead, present or absent from the physical household. The key is that they be image-bearing personifications of competing identity claims. In structural-analytic theory the conflict or stress in the dyad that eventuates in a symptom-bearing or problem-carrying third person is always a conflict over competing identity claims. Developmental arrest is an unresolved image struggle.

Developmental Tasks

Most attempts to understand development and the family life cycle begin with variations of Duvall's (1977) stages, which, as Carter and McGoldrick (1980) pointed out, address "nodal events related to the comings and goings of family members: the birth and raising of children, the departure of children from the household, retirement and death'' (p. 6). Approaching development from a conceptual angle different from Duvall's sociological perspective, structural analysis focuses on a set of boundary-shaping tasks and the dilemmas these pose for the couple whose primary system function is to establish a family model or paradigm to guide family members. These tasks are

1. attachment, making a commitment to another person and discovering the rules and boundaries of the relationship.
2. industry, developing strategies for getting things done, inside and outside the family, without compromising individual needs.
3. affiliation, extending commitments outward to extended family, institutions, organizations, and others.
4. inclusion, allowing others to be brought within the family boundaries to share its resources, affections, and identity. Mostly, of course, this refers to children.
5. centralization (a task that overlaps the others), consolidating the accomplishments and gains made from the facing of other tasks. It may take many years to elaborate already established structures for meeting new contingencies.
6. decentralization, loosening boundaries to let people out. Especially, this refers to children leaving home. Like centralization, this may occur over many years, starting with the departure of the first member and lasting until the last member sets out on an independent path.
7. differentiation, each member of the couple addressing the needs of self-actualization, individual uniqueness, and individualization without compromising what is right about the union or undoing the individual's attachment to it.
8. detachment, letting go, terminating a couple arrangement (as in divorce), dissolving ties (as in a political defection or the breaking up of a commune), approaching death and sharing these matters within the couple or family unit.

These eight developmental tasks are the larger culture's value prescriptions, its recommendations as to what its members are to be concerned about on the operations level. For example, the larger culture expects members of would-be families to court, form intimate relationships, and eventually marry. The ways in which the tasks are actually dealt with to establish family structures, however, are mediated by idiosyncratic subcultural family and individual influences. In regard to the task of attachment, for example, many female members of the poor culture in the United States skip the courting aspects of intimate commitments and begin their families without a husband. Their middle-class counterparts may live with men they never marry, while each individual pursues a career. These family forms represent family systems approaching the developmental tasks in a different order and in different ways.

Crises can occur around any of the eight developmental tasks. Each task raises a focal issue and a dilemma. Attachment, for example, raises the issues of commitment, loyalty, trust, or sexual passion and the dilemma of twoness versus oneness. The focal issue is the cultural source of family system crisis, growth, and change. While systems can grow without crisis, more radical changes begin with crisis. For example, when a couple's images are compatible around inclusion, a task in which the focal issue is whether and how to include and grow inward and the dilemma is the availability versus the depletion of personal resources, they may readily agree to have their first child between the 2nd and 3rd year of their marriage. If the images or the image elements are competitive, however, as when the man's image does not prepare him for sharing affection or the woman's image calls for a career before motherhood while for her mate the reverse order holds, a crisis may ensue in which images of inclusion compete with images of industry.

Thus, a developmental crisis occurs when the following conditions prevail:

1. The culture to which the couple subscribes endows one of the eight developmental tasks with a value prescription whose implied mandate enjoins the couple to respond. ("People should court before marriage." "People should not engage in sex before marriage." "Married people should have children." "Women with infant children should not work." "People should mourn the death of a loved one.")
2. The couple recognizes the validity of the prescription and its enjoinment. (People are, or become members of, subcultures with values different from those of the larger culture. In some subcultures the precursor to marriage is "getting pregnant" rather than "courting," couples decide on political and ideological grounds not to have children, women bring their children to work, and mourning is a casual event or an elaborate ritual.)
3. Each partner experiences the surfacing of a critical image whose elements clash with the others, leading to competing identity claims and a *potential* developmental crisis. (If the culture fails to inspire an

image of importance in one partner, there is a small potential for crisis in the couple system. If the couple's images are compatible with one another and with the culture, there is similarly no basis for crisis between the partners or between the partners and the cultural community. The potential for crisis becomes real and manifest when a struggle over competing identity claims and claims on reality ensues and persists.

4. Within the couple system and its already established structure, the "steering mechanisms" (Kantor, 1980), a special set of mechanisms available for problem-solving and crisis resolution, break down. (In some systems the steering mechanisms are generally weak, in others generally strong, and in most systems, weak for some and for new circumstances.)

When all four of the above conditions are present, the couple's unsuccessful efforts to resolve their conflict eventuates in a ritual impasse, the so-called redundancy that bogs the system down developmentally, claims individual casualties through symptom formation or problem behavior, and, in increasing instances, leads to disassembling of families or to divorce (Kantor & Vickers, 1983).

Stages of Therapy

In structural analysis, therapy is divided into three stages, and techniques are strictly geared to the realization of stage-related goals. In the first stage, the goal is always problem relief; in the second, transformation of disabled structures underlying the system disablement; and in the third, prevention of future disablement by involving in the therapy family members associated with the next most vulnerable structure.

There are eight steps or procedures that a therapist who remains with a family through the three stages of therapy would follow (Kantor, 1980; Kantor & Barnett, 1979):

Stage 1: Symptom relief or problem resolution
   Step 1. Locating the key ritual sequence
   Step 2. Isolating the psychopolitical configuration and making preliminary changes in these
   Step 3. Eliciting the competing critical identity images

Stage 2: Transformation of underlying structures that fuel and maintain the symptom or problem
  Step 4. Pinning down the image elements and their interaction
  Step 5. Fixing the images
  Step 6. Transforming images into positive identity claims
Stage 3: Prevention of symptom recurrence in the next most vulnerable structure.
  Step 7. Sharing the theory
  Step 8. Generalizing the theory to the next most vulnerable members

As with most systems therapies, "success" in the structural-analytic approach occurs with a restructuring of behavior (Step 2) and of perspective (Step 3). In contrast with some systems approaches, however, new perspective is gained in the structural-analytic approach through direct reframing, when each partner's competing image is brought to the surface of awareness and shared. With this restructuring, the goals of Stage 1 are reached.

In therapy conducted in the developmental perspective, the family *if it chooses*, is assisted in dealing with the underlying structure that fueled and maintained the symptom or problem that brought the family into therapy in the first place. It is here that the assumption made by many systems therapists—that symptom relief or problem resolution automatically puts the family developmentally back on track—is empirically tested. Stages 2 and 3 are designed for those clinical situations in which this assumption is proved incorrect. Indeed, effective work in Stage 2 permits the therapist to identify the next most vulnerable structure, which often makes it possible to predict the next casualty and to do preventive therapy earmarked for particular family members whose potential incapacitation is an indication that the family's developmental course has not yet been corrected.

THE TREATMENT OF DEVELOPMENTAL CRISES: A SUMMARY

Therapy with the Rostows has been conducted from the developmental perspective of structural-analytic theory. Three subunits have been seen in four therapy sequences—Denise and her mother; Maryanne and William, as a couple; Maryanne, William, and Elaine; and, currently, Maryanne and William once again.

Treatment of the Mother-Daughter Dyad

In the first therapy with the Rostows, the "couple" was Maryanne and her mother, who was not physically present. The triangulated members were the daughter, 17-year-old Denise, and father. Therapy ended after the first stage, with relief of Denise's symptoms (mild disassociation, marked indecision about career choice, identity confusion, and ideational preoccupation) and with repair of the disabled system structure (mother-daughter fusion, in which each was acting to remain enmeshed with the other, while protesting this deep involvement, and a peripheralized though concerned father, William, was not permitted to help). Two years later, Denise remained symptom-free, and a new structure was intact.

The effectiveness of this therapy was based on two features of correct diagnostic process—accurate identification both of the "couple" involved in the identity struggle and of the developmental task that was being addressed. After one long meeting with the entire family, the therapist saw, in sequences of varying lengths, Denise alone, Denise with her mother, Denise with her mother and father, and another extended meeting with the entire family, engineered and brilliantly choreographed by Denise. The developmental task was identified as decentralization. Maryanne and Denise had been strongly bonded from the start and had enjoyed an essentially trouble-free relationship until Denise's adolescence and imminent launching. It became clear in the therapy that, in facing her daughter's leaving, Maryanne was resurrecting her heretofore unaddressed hurt and confusion at being launched far too gladly by a mother with whom she had a close relationship, although this relationship was based more on a shared anger at father-husband than on a true bonding. Confusion around the dilemma of this developmental task, loss versus gain, was being passed on by mother to daughter, who, along with William, was being triangulated into an unacknowledged identity struggle.

Key to the repair of the fused structure were two enactment techniques: (1) a sculpture involving Maryanne and her symbolically represented mother, with Denise as an active bystander; (2) a series of role reversals in which mother and daughter played the three women interchangeably in contexts designed to get at issues of autonomy and emotional distance (alternately too close and too distant in Maryanne's experience with her mother, amounting to a subtle abandonment and "not caring"; and so consistently close in Denise's experience as to cause a confusion of personal boundaries and a guilt-producing sense of too great caring).

Also important to the restructuring of the family's dysfunctional action structures was a carefully timed homework assignment wherein Denise with her mother's support invited her father to an elegant Saturday brunch at the Ritz, paid for with her own earnings. Such an exercise is a structural remodeling, the design of which is based on an articulated analysis of the structure of key elements of the involved images, including of course "missing elements." Through the brunch assignment, Maryanne was overtly supporting (following), rather than covertly undermining (opposing), close experiences between father and daughter; Denise was moving to reward her father, giving rather than thanklessly taking and/or critically demanding (a paradoxical reversal that resulted in William subsequently taking initiatives to contact his daughter); and Maryanne was coming to a beginning awareness of her identity struggle with her own mother, issues that she had assiduously avoided both in life and in her therapy.

This 6-month, 15-session therapy was punctuated at termination by a ritual celebration of Denise's coming of age as a young woman, officially to announce her decision to put off attending the college she had been admitted to for a year of work in Israel. Systemically, it amounted to an announcement of her detriangulation and separation from her enmeshed family.

Treatment of the Adult Couple: First Course

Three months after therapy with the mother-daughter dyad was terminated, William and Maryanne came for therapy. (Denise, in her ritual celebration, had prescribed therapy for her parents.) The problem was, in their language, "total noncommunication," a sense of "alienation," Maryanne's "spiraling anxiety and off-the-wallness," and William's "unavailability and complete failure to follow through on his parenting responsibilities." (They were also sexually abstinent and had been for many years, though, as many couples do, they denied this during their first course of therapy.) In the present vocabulary, theirs was a problem around issues of attachment that ran so deep as to contaminate most of their efforts to reconcile differences, even insignificant ones, associated with other developmental tasks. Interestingly, their problems did not surface in connection with Denise, but began to appear more in connection with Charles and were clear in connection with Elaine.

The first attempt to treat the intimate dyad was not successful. The rule—select techniques designed to eliminate the symptom or resolve the problem before shifting to techniques better suited to transformation—did not succeed here.

This generally occurs when one or both partners in the marital dyad have individual developmental issues that run deep, have been distortedly projected onto the couple relationship, and have not surfaced in the therapy. In short, the developmental diagnosis was incomplete. The "couple" whose images were at issue *was* William and Maryanne, which is not always the case in couples therapy. The developmental task at which they were stuck *was* attachment. The focal issues were commitment and intimacy; the dilemma was loneliness versus invasiveness. Because Elaine's antics at home, at school, and in the community escalated to crisis levels that surpassed those of the couple's problems, the deep sexual alienation of Maryanne and William and the depth of personal injury each felt in connection with the missing elements in the images they reported were not discovered at this time. Perhaps, as systems therapists believe, there may have been a relationship between the couple's minor successes in dealing with their attachment issues and the episodic escalations of Elaine's bizarre behaviors and threatened hospitalization. In any event, when these behaviors could not be ignored the focus of therapy was shifted from the couple to the pathological triad.

Treatment of the Pathological Triad

These three did appear crazy. Maryanne was a specimen of anxiety-ridden fatigue from being on a constant alert, dogging every breath and step 14-year-old Elaine made or threatened to make. Elaine could not have been more inventive in discovering ways to push her mother over the edge—using alcohol and drugs exhibitionistically, begging for money at the Mall, having secret rendezvous in the middle of the night with discredited local youths, engaging in sex in public places. In the brief intervals between these intrepid provocations, she was a sensitive, needy 6 year old. Maryanne, ludicrously tightening her unworkable controls, demanded help from William, who characteristically followed a course of impotent restraint until either mother or daughter in their different ways insisted on relief. Then, desperate, he clumsily assumed the posture of the despot or the actively concerned parent—retrieving Elaine after she had run away, confronting her at some wild party, meeting endlessly with school officials or with Elaine's psychiatrist, who was proposing hospitalization. Not unexpectedly, when the dust had settled, mother and daughter were secretly joined in a negative coalition, ridiculing William's efforts as "too little and too late."

The treatment goals were to stabilize executive authority by getting the parents to cooperate, block Elaine from dividing them, relocate Elaine in the power hierarchy, mend the affectual split in the couple subsystem (which was responsible for their refusal to join cooperatively in parenting), prevent Maryanne from undermining the very authority she insisted William exercise, and block William from almost intentionally "striking out" so that Maryanne would no longer be forced to "pinch hit." The more practical goals were to avoid Elaine's hospitalization (her mother, father, psychiatrist, and Elaine herself were at various times convinced there was no other course), reduce if not eliminate her runaways, and bring her intractability under parental control and self-control.

While the practical goals were reached in a course of therapy that has lasted 8 months, it was not easy and it is not over.

Therapy was made difficult not by Elaine's intractability, which was considerable, but by the couple's. Every time they came close to bringing things under control, one or the other would sabotage the effort. They seemed resolute, cooperation meaning defeat. A form of modified couples therapy was adopted, along with the child-centered therapy, as assurance to the parents that they would not be required to sacrifice their selves and sense of reality for their child.

There was one other problem in planning treatment for this unit—neurological involvement in Elaine's behavior and school performance. Two weeks following her birth, Elaine saw a specialist for a suspected convulsion. She has seen specialists for suspected deficits at every turning point in her life, learning disability the only one that has been definitively established.

Elaine also suffered a psychological deficit from birth. Given the status of the marriage relationship at the time of Elaine's accidental birth, Maryanne wanted nothing less than a third child. She simply withdrew her affection and nurturance.

Crucial to reaching the goals of Stage 1 with the Rostows was the proper developmental diagnosis. This subunit suffered from a massive profusion of failed and failing efforts to evolve system level strategies for helping Elaine at *each* critical juncture throughout her individual developmental history. At root were (a) the specific competing images of each parent, the elements of which remained essentially untransformed because of an early emotional-sexual divorce, (b) leading to a chronic developmental breakdown, primarily around issues of attachment and secondarily around issues of inclusion and industry, (c) resulting in a series of disabled structures to deal with nurturance, a sense of being cared for, and a sense of competency, principally involving and affecting the couple's last, unwanted, child, (d) whose possible neurological deficits (requiring more rather than less able parenting) served as a vehicle for the couple both covertly continuing their image battle and overtly avoiding the seriousness of their emotional and physical disaffection.

A breakthrough in the therapy occurred in one of the couple sessions when they were required to talk with one another not about their troubles with Elaine, but about their "divorce." ("You two divorced on your honeymoon and have never quite faced it.") Startled, but in complete agreement, they began to discuss it both in and out of sessions, with these apparent results. They sustained civilized, though not always intimate, communication for weeks. They began to divide tasks in connection with Elaine's difficulties without sabotaging the arrangement. They produced additional memories that showed how their competing images and the missing elements contributed to the dysfunctional structures they had created in their relationship and in their dealings with Elaine. Key to the stabilizing of parental control were the new ways they were negotiating over the distribution of nurturing and competency-giving responsibilities in connection with Elaine and her problems, which by no means were totally eliminated, although the running away and bizarre behaviors were.

Treatment of the Adult Couple: Second Course

It was learned only during the second course of therapy that the "divorce" was not merely emotional. It was physical. William and Maryanne had not made love or enjoyed sex together in over 14 years. In the course of pinning down the image elements, it was learned that Maryanne had become physically ill, and, failing to recognize her need for nurturance, William had offered her sex instead "with such dumb persistence that almost instantly my heart went cold." Thereafter such "disappointments" (recall her image) were experienced with deadening frequency, but only once as profoundly as on the honeymoon. Soon after Charles' birth, Maryanne, distressed over her child's constant crying, telephoned William who was away on a business trip and asked him to return immediately. When he did not, their sexual divorce was sealed. Discovering that nothing he did thereafter would please his wife (recall his image), William "buried his fury," retreated psychologically to his basement, and directed his energies elsewhere, hoping to please by succeeding in the world. Over the next 18 years, experts of all kinds (psychoanalysts, pediatricians, neurologists, psychologists, school counselors, endocrinologists, and now a family therapist) were drawn in, almost as part of the family. Their assignment and system function was to supply the missing elements, the wished for redemptive acts in each partner's original foundation event, still untransformed into positive identity claims, and, therefore, still the potential source of future system disablements based on new competing image struggles.

CONCLUSION

Therapy can help William and Maryanne with their individual developmental tasks, although they may not reach a level of intimacy even approaching their premarital expectations. Whatever the outcome, the couple will be better armed structurally for more effective parenting.

It appears that the next most vulnerable structures involve Charles and Elaine at future junctures in the family developmental cycle. Elaine, only now receiving the unfiltered nurturing and care she should have received as an infant and child, may not be ready for a "launching" in two or three years, nor will her mother. Charles, who has been spared Elaine's systemic catastrophes of late, may not survive as well later. Since his first, early bout with the family's damaged attachment structures, he has managed by substituting the rewards of achievement and competency for the rewards of emotional closeness and intimacy. However, one must speculate that, after succeeding at college and launching a career, he may encounter difficulties when taking on the tasks of intimate relationships. ("I have never had a truly intimate relationship in my life," his father confessed recently.)

REFERENCES

Carter, E.A., & McGoldrick, M. *The family life cycle: A framework for family therapy.* New York: Gardner Press, 1980.

Duvall, E. *Marriage and family development* (5th ed.). Philadelphia: Lippincott, 1977.

Haley, J. *Uncommon therapy: The psychiatric techniques of Milton H. Erickson.* New York: Norton, 1973.

Kantor, D., & Lehr, W. *Inside the family.* San Francisco: Jossey Bass, 1975.

Kantor, D. Critical identity image: A concept linking individual, couple and family development. In J.K. Pearce & L.J. Friedman (Eds.), *Family therapy: Combining psychodynamic and family systems approaches.* New York: Grune & Stratton, 1980.

Kantor, D., & Barnett, J.G. *Image and identity: A videotape course on Dr. David Kantor's theories of couple and family therapy.* Cambridge, MA: M.I.T., 1979.

Kantor, D., Lebow, D., & Cameron, J. *I and we: A videotape presentation of David Kantor's concept—Critical identity image.* Boston: University of Massachusetts, 1977.

Kantor, D., & Troupmann, J. The genesis of systems, in process.

Kantor, D., & Vickers, M. Divorce along the family life cycle. In H. Liddle (ed.), *Clinical implications of the family life cycle.* Rockville, MD: Aspen Systems Corporation, 1983.

3. The Family Life Cycle and Families with Young Children

Lee Combrinck-Graham, MD
Director
Masters in Family Therapy Program
Associate Professor
Mental Health Sciences
Hahnemann University
Philadelphia, Pennsylvania

One morning recently I awakened at 5:30 to the sound of someone in the bathroom. It was my 5-year-old son relieving himself. I waited quietly, listening. He finished, and I heard him padding back to his room. Would the light snap on? No. Would the record player suddenly blare, "Ladies and Gentlemen, Birds, and Monsters . . ."? No. He had gone back to bed. He had simply taken care of his need without involving me, his mother, in any way. It was a milestone.

I read often that one of the hallmarks of a healthy family is the presence of clear boundaries, for it is in the distinctions between people's selves that intimacy can be experienced. I believed this, myself, before I became a parent. Now, however, I think that these beliefs are held by adults who have observed families in which the children are far more differentiated and independent than is the youngster in the bathroom that recent morning. These adult observers describe youngsters with the experience and cognitive complexity to perceive themselves and their worlds in their own ways. They describe children who do not need someone to interpret for them, to tell them if the soup is too hot or if they should wear their galoshes, or to explain that they cannot expect to marry Mommy and never have any more school.

Soon my son will be 15, and I will again believe in interpersonal boundaries as the panacea for healthy family life. I must try to capture some of the experiences around the time my son was born before they slip away forever. When he was born, I was propelled on a wave of exhilaration for days. I could not sleep and would often get up to watch both my son and his father sleeping as if there were nothing more important to do. I was emotional and focused. I jerked every jerk for him; I scrutinized every cry, every sigh, every coo, every twist of his mouth. We fought. We fought in his very first day. He had trouble learning how to nurse, and so did I, so we fought about it until we learned. We went to work together, we came home together, we sang together. When he was 5 weeks old, he went to stay with another person during the day while I went to work. I cannot describe the pain I experienced when I tore myself away from him that day, and the next, and the next. It must have been the pain of building an interpersonal boundary.

My husband used to hold our son on his lap at the table and bounce his hands and legs on the table, singing a song as if Mark were playing it on the piano or conducting it. When he was 5 weeks old, he smiled at this, letting his arms and legs be danced over the table. Sometimes, there were flourishes and pretend chords, fortissimo, at the lower register. At the end, there were bows and applause. At 1, he gave his own concerts on the harpsichord, complete with flourish and low chord; when he learned the word, he demanded, "Clap." When his father conducted a small ensemble, Mark stood in the back and helped, following the performance with abundant bows and applause. At first, father and son were as one in an activity through which an interpersonal boundary has developed so that they do their different things together.

I am the parent of a 5-year-old with a wild imagination. Sometimes, the things he says simply do not go together. I feel that I have to understand what he means, often when he is just experimenting and does not know what he means himself. I feel that I have to help him ground his ideas and make sense out of them without losing the freshness and originality of his thoughts. But that is what I have to do, now. Last month, I had to get up to help him to the bathroom. Now, I do not have to do that.

The periods of family life in which the children are young form several arcs of the family life cycle. The characteristics of families in these periods depend not only on the presence of young children, but also on the reciprocal interactions of all the generations in the family. Ideally, the family provides a context suited to the development of all its members. Although certain characteristics of a particular family may be ideal for some individuals or generations, these conditions are not always ideal for others in the family. Then a compromise must be struck. This state of compromise and the flexibility to adjust characterize the healthy family.

A MODEL OF FAMILY SYSTEM CHANGE THROUGH THE LIFE CYCLE

Development is a distinctly linear concept, unidirectional and epigenetic. Most developmentalists argue for an invariable sequence of unfolding developmental stages. For example, a human life begins with conception and ends with death. The life of the family is not linear, however; it does not begin or end, but continues with the deaths of some members and the births of others. Designations of "young" or "older" families usually refer to the status of the children in the family. Frequently, these categorizations do not address the family as a system with membership beyond a household and with all its "intergenerational connectedness" (McGoldrick & Carter, 1982).

Consistent with the notion that families, as systems, have nonlinear courses, the term *family life cycle* is a useful descriptor. It refers to the repetitive, recycling set of configurations and issues through which the family passes. These configurations and issues often correspond with life events of the individuals in the family and with their development. It is possible to define some characteristics of the changing relationship system over the course of the family life cycle.

Figure 1 presents sets of individual life events or developmental stages in relationship with one another in a family so that they appear in a spiral. The ideal relationships depicted suggest that there is a harmony and developmental reciprocity when, for example, generativity in adults coincides with the birth and childhood of their offspring and when the adolescence of children coincides with the 40s reevaluation of their parents. In the first instance, the family is most *centripetal,* or cohesive, as represented by compression at the top of Figure 1. In the second case, the family is most *centrifugal,* as represented by the expansion of the curves at the bottom of Figure 1. Those reciprocal developmental points in the middle fall between the centripetal and centrifugal systems, when the system is moving from one to the other and making the attendant shifts in organization, configurations, and boundaries.

Figure 1 Family Life Spiral

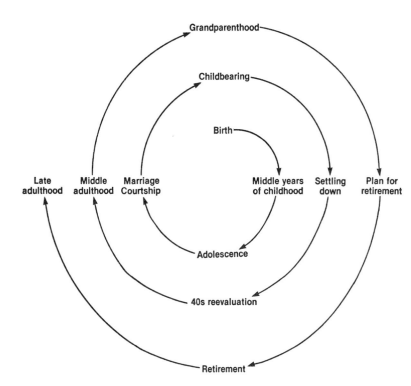

Centripetal and centrifugal? In physics, centripetal and centrifugal forces usually oppose each other, as when they hold the planets in orbit. As they are metaphorically applied to families, they are seen as unbalanced, with one or the other predominating. Beavers (1982) described centripetal and centrifugal systems as follows: "Centripetal family members look for gratification predominantly from within the family and are less trustful of the world beyond the family boundaries. . . . Centrifugal families, on the contrary, expect gratification from beyond the family and trust activities and relationships outside the family unit more than within it" (p. 57). Centripetal families are seen as "enmeshed," and centrifugal families are seen as "disengaged." The terms *enmeshed* and *disengaged* define the boundary characteristics of a family system. An enmeshed system has diffuse interpersonal boundaries within the system, but a firm boundary around it; a disengaged system is likely to have the reverse.

These terms, then, are not descriptions of pathological organization, but of relationship styles within the family. Beavers found in his studies of families of adolescents that, with a knowledge of the type of organization (i.e., centripetal or centrifugal) and family dysfunction, it is possible to predict the kind of psychopathology that may be found in the family. If the predominance of force is centripetal at a time in the family life cycle when the family should be coming apart, or vice versa, the family is likely to experience dysfunction. For example, the battle about weight, appearance, and food in families with an anorectic adolescent is often a battle fought in a centripetal system that should be coming apart. The 4-year-old who wreaks destruction while the parents stand by wringing their hands and marveling at the child's will lives in a system that should be more centripetal.

If the same family system is observed over a long period of time, it can be seen that the boundaries shift in a regular and predictable fashion. In families with very young children, the boundaries are quite strong around the family and quite permeable within it. There is a high degree of responsiveness between individuals in the family at all generational levels, which could be described as normal, healthy enmeshment. When the youngest generation completes the launching process, the boundaries around the family are often difficult to define, while the interpersonal boundaries between family members are very clear; individuation and personal identity become issues for all.

There are several important implications of the family life cycle. First, family health over time is a reflection of the family's ability to adjust its configuration to the changing needs of its members. The family should be able to change its boundaries as the life cycle evolves. Second, developmental misfit, the condition in which the family is out of phase with the development of its individual members, is a major factor in symptom formation. Another view of the relationship between life cycle events and the onset of symptoms was proposed by Haley (1973), who described crises at transitional points. Third, in addition to the suitability of the centripetal or centrifugal environment for individual developmental tasks, the fact that the family system may cycle three times from one pole to the other in the lifetime of an individual suggests that there are important family experiences to be gained in these different contexts. These experiences might be understood as the practicing of intimacy in the centripetal phases and of individuation in the centrifugal ones. Fourth, modern families often appear to be collages of generations applied to one another. Yet, they adapt to the demands of their individuals' developmental tasks.

Becoming a Centripetal Family

After adolescents grow to be young adults and leave home, the family passes the most centrifugal period of its cycle. Following what is almost a dissolution of the family system, with the children leaving and the parents reassessing their own marriages, careers, and life directions, there comes another settling down period. As the younger generation courts, the older generation also reassesses relationships. After disengagement, this period of the family life cycle is like rapprochement.

Friedman (1980) described celebrations and family rites of passage to reflect the process that the family has been undergoing. A wedding signals the ritual coming together of families. In choosing a mate from their own peer group, the offspring can reapproach their parents without danger of being reabsorbed into the child role. At a wedding, parents often say that they have not lost a child, but have gained one.

This proves to be true because, ritually, not only the couple and the two families come together, but also each family is once again drawn together. A wedding, the ceremonial end of these individuals' search for a partner, an intimate relationship, and the status to form a nuclear family of their own, marks a major step in the motion of the family toward a centripetal system.

Being a Centripetal Family

A centripetal family is focused primarily on events occurring within the family itself. There is a strong boundary around the outside of the family, while boundaries within it are generally fluid. Although parents in a centripetal family have a strong sense of their roles as parents, they often respond to the infant in a quite undifferentiated way. This periodic blending of wills and persons allows family members to act in each other's behalf, often without a specific request or even a conscious acknowledgment of the need. For example, the mother knows the meaning of her infant's cry. This same kind of responsiveness occurs between husband and wife as they, often wordlessly, move to help each other, as well as between grandparents and parents in these systems.

The enmeshed quality of the centripetal family is shown clearly by the activity in the family of a new baby. The grandparents travel long distances to see the new grandchild and to help the new parents. The father rushes home from work to play with the baby before the baby goes to sleep. Bleary-eyed parents are up half the night straining to satisfy this mysterious being so they can all sleep; they grope their way through the day, preparing for another night of intensity with their infant. Three areas of study underscore this enmeshed quality of the family at this time: attachment (Bowlby, 1969), bonding (Kennel & Klaus, 1976), and separation and individuation (Bergman, Mahler, & Pine, 1975).

Attachment is the process by which a new individual establishes a relationship with another person. The attachment figure becomes an indispensable provider of structure, nurturance, and meaning to the infant. When an attachment object is lost, despair may be so great as to cause extreme discomfort and decline. The Robertsons' film of the stages of protest, withdrawal, and despair of a toddler whose mother leaves for another confinement is a striking presentation of the effects of loss of an attachment figure (1967).

The work done on bonding has focused on the forces that bind the parent to the child. Most investigators have described mother-infant bonding, although some have also described how the ecstasy or altered state that occurs at a birth captures the attention and affection of all who are involved and creates a susceptibility in them for bonding to the infant. Bonding affects the responsiveness of parents to their children over at least the first 5 years. Some of the research demonstrated, for example, that there is a higher incidence of child abuse in families in which there had been some interference in the bonding process.

The names of Mahler's early stages of separation and individuation are autism and symbiosis. The terms illustrate the infant's psychological fusion to the mother. Although Mahler does not describe the reciprocal responses of the mother in the same terms, the often reported sense of physical pain described by mothers when they leave their infants for the first time may reflect the mothers' symbiotic fusion to their babies, as well.

Unfortunately, most of this work concerns the mother-child relationship exclusively and does not consider the family as a system. Bowlby observed that other family members may become secondary attachment figures, or even primary attachment figures if the mother is not immediately available. Engrossment, a kind of altered perception in the fathers of newborns, is described in one of the infrequent studies on the relationships between fathers and their new offspring (Greenberg & Morris, 1974). Research on the transformation of marital relationships and changes in sexual patterns after childbirth tends to focus on what is lost rather than on what is gained between the adults in this period. The more differentiated functions of the couple without children are lost, but the almost indescribable altered state renders the individuals receptive to intense intimacy. This may appear as a kind of ecstasy or emotionality that, in mothers, may be attributed to anesthesia or hormones. What hormones would produce similar states in fathers and grandparents, however? What hormones account for Margaret Mead's response to her grandchild, "I had never thought how strange it was to be *involved* at a distance in the birth of a biological descendant . . . the extraordinary sense of having been *transformed*" (emphasis added; Walsh, 1980, p. 204)? Whatever the cause, these states produce the loss of boundaries, the helplessness to explain, and an availability of the individual selves within the family system which allows for a profound intimacy.

The birth of a child is a trigger in a family that, because it has been coming together since the courtship period and marriage, is prepared for this event. Other events, such as the purchase of a house, may trigger similar emotionality, but the birth of a baby seems to be the most profound of these events. Furthermore, the centripetal family is the most suitable context for the infant's early development, for an infant needs the kind of responsiveness and intuitive understanding that characterize this kind of family.

Becoming a Centrifugal Family

The unfolding of the centripetal family system as it moves, once again, toward a centrifugal configuration can correspond with the gradual individuation of a child in the family. For example, the early delicate combination of responsiveness and differentiation associated with the child's development of language normally occurs within the essentially centripetal family context. The child's earliest experiments with language may not communicate much, but they are enthusiastically received by the family so that the child is encouraged to experiment further. The father of a 13-month-old recently reported that his child's favorite word was "vacuum cleaner," which the child refers to as "Ba." A child's babbling at this point is incomprehensible to anyone but a family member. Later, the child takes off in the thrill of language, the sound, the music, and the wonderful adventures it can describe. A child can say what he believes and believe what he says. The involved family continues to know what is meant, encouraging the joyful play with language and grounding the expressions in real experience. These are functions, for the child, of a family that is still centripetal in its preoccupations with its members, but is developing more distinguishable interpersonal boundaries.

By the time the children are school-aged, the family has made a definite shift toward a more differentiated system. The family members, like planets, may spin in orbits that seem more distinct from each other, but centripetal forces are still strong enough to keep the family members in a structured relationship to one another. The family system is not yet ready to come apart. The family in this phase is fluid in its ecology, reopening itself to the effects of the larger society.

New ideas and perspectives begin to enter into the family system. Outsiders are allowed into the family in greater numbers, and family members who venture outside the system take a new, critical view of their own family. Children come home from school with comments on how teachers and other children's parents do things. Sullivan (1953) hails the "juvenile era" of childhood as that period when at last society can modify the family's influence on the child.

This period of childhood often corresponds to the so-called settling down period in adulthood (Levinson, 1978). This occurs in the mid-30s and is characterized by adult efforts to establish a "niche in society" and to work at "advancement." Personal tasks for adults in this era of the family life cycle are in harmony with the children's tasks of self-development through schooling. The adults are occupied with their professional development or, in the case of nonworking parents, their roles in relationship to other parents. Through the school contacts of their children alone, parents and their values are reflected in a way that results in a conscious modification. Processes of feedback and modification aid working parents' quest to advance themselves and establish a professional identity.

The grandparent generation, too, participates in this general family interest in the surrounding society. Having already established places for themselves, grandparents may be redefining their relationships with the larger society (Levinson, 1978) in yet another way. Politics, philanthropic activities, and social groups or clubs may occupy more of their time. A relationship with the grandchildren can provide even greater exposure for each as the children are now independent enough to accompany the grandparents on outings.

At all generational levels of such a family there are consistency and reciprocity. The children's contacts at school expose the parents to redefining elements in the larger society, while the parents' greater concern with personal development frees the children for further explorations outside the family. The family in this phase is engaged in the simultaneous processes of living with its own structure and grounding it firmly while changing it in response to greater social exposure. It is like a house in the summertime, sturdy, but with doors and windows open for free circulation. All come in to share a family meal, to take shelter in the rain, and to sleep. It is a practicing period for individuals, living within a structure that is to be abandoned, dismantled, or renovated in the next phase of the life cycle.

EXCEPTIONS TO THE MODEL

The model described illustrates a synchronous opening and closing of family relationship patterns as the family moves through the life cycle. In a model family system in which the generations are separated by about 25 years, the centripetal or centrifugal nature of the family context is suitable for all generations at the same time. Because many families do not have this arrangement of generations, oscillations between centripetal and centrifugal states are not always as neat as the model represents.

It is clear that a centripetal family is the best context for young children. Major exceptions to the model of the cozy centripetal family of the neonate are observed when the family members cannot come together in a traditional way, for example, when the parents are not married and do not live together, when the parents are adolescent, when the parents are much older than most parents, and when the parents have been married to others in the past.

Alone, the birth of an infant may not cause the family system to come together, even though the centripetal system is the best for infant development. The family context of an infant born to a single mother depends on the developmental circumstances of the mother and her family. If the mother is in her 30s, has chosen to become a parent, and has thought through the balance of child care and breadwinning responsibilities, the family is likely to have the enmeshed qualities of the centripetal system, although the components may include grandparents or nonrelated care-givers. If, on the other hand, the single mother is a teen-ager in a precarious position in her own family—poised for leaving—she is not likely to have the resources to enfold the infant into an enmeshing environment. It is, however, possible that her parents can take charge of the infant as one of their own, thus postponing for themselves the issues of the centrifugal period. Such an arrangement can provide a supportive context for the mother to nurture her own baby, or it can allow the mother to pursue her own developmental course. The following examples illustrate two different arrangements addressing the issue.

Ms. C is now 22 and has a 4-year-old son. The child's father is in prison. Ms. C and her son live with her 8-year-old sister and her parents. They share a bed in a single room. Her son was premature, and he remained in the hospital for 4½ months after his birth. Ms. C was with him night and day for that period. She is very attached to him. As the child grew older, he developed pretty well, but he was sickly, having a chronic lung condition. He also failed to develop normal language. Finally, at the urging of her parents, Ms. C placed him in a special school when he was 3½. This was their first experience away from each other. Now her parents (possibly because of their own readiness for greater differentiation) would like her to do something with her life, and she would like to move out of her parents' home and be independent. She reports arguments with her father, who wants her to establish some direction for her life.

In this family, an intimate and supportive context was provided for the mother and her fragile baby. The system finally began to open up. The mother's sister was school-aged, her son began school, and the entire family is now addressing issues of differentiation

Elizabeth is 16. When she was born, her mother was 14, and her father was 17. They were not married, and she went to live with her paternal grandparents when she was 4 months old because her mother was not able to care for her. Except for a year ago, when she lived with her mother for a few months, Elizabeth has lived with her grandparents all her life. Her father lived separately, but he would come home to discipline her when summoned by his parents. He, now 33, is married to a 22-year-old woman. Elizabeth feels that her stepmother is too close to her own age. She resents her stepmother, and she fears that her father and stepmother will have a baby whom they will love more than they love her.

Grandparents had stepped in to raise a baby for whom neither parent could care. The father's responsibility to the child was maintained by assigning disciplinary tasks to him, but otherwise he was free to pursue his own personal development. He is now entering into a natural family sequence with his own wife. Elizabeth feels that she belongs to no one and looks longingly at the cohesion of her father's marriage from the perspective of her own increasing differentiation.

In each of these two cases, the family provided a significant resource to the parents and baby. The extended family unit was flexible enough to provide the centripetal, nurturant context best for the infant. In the first case, this enabled the mother, too, to involve herself with the infant, temporarily postponing her own differentiation. In the other case, it enabled the parents to continue with their differentiation.

If the family into which a baby is born has older children and is a family system in the centrifugal period, there is another kind of challenge to the system; this family must cleave to the baby and continue the processes of differentiation at the same time. Members of large families frequently stay very much more attached to each other than do members of smaller ones. The older children may not leave the family as early as the youngsters in other families do, or, if they do leave, they marry and live in the area. In a sense, the births of successive children tend to keep the family in a prolonged centripetal state. Adolescent children in such a system deal normally with their individual development in the family, often by participating in the adult functions of caring for younger children, which maintains their investment in the family while they mature and prepare themselves to establish a family of their own.

A remarried family is defined as a system in which one or both of the spouses were previously married with children. The family relationships in a remarried family that produces its own children are extremely complicated. For example, the husband with his college-aged children and their mother comprise family A. The wife with her school-aged children and their father comprise family B. As family systems, including the grandparents, families A and B have each experienced the centripetal period when the children were born, and they have moved through the period of opening up in the children's school years. Family A became centrifugal, and it was in this period that the marriage dissolved, as a natural consequence, in that family, of the centrifugal forces. Family B broke up in an earlier period of its life cycle. Mr. A and Mrs. B marry and form a new system, C. Then they have children, becoming family C. The children of families A and B may relate to the C household, but, remaining members of families A and B, continue their own courses. The A children continue the centrifugal motion of their own family, and the B children continue to move in that direction, too, but are a step behind in the life cycle. All of this goes on while Mr. and Mrs. C enter into a new centripetal phase through their remarriage and the birth of their baby. Family C has the delicate task of allowing the A children to differentiate and leave, being an open structure for the B children, and having strong centripetal forces around the baby.

There are also exceptions to the model family with school-aged children, in which the individuals at all generations have achieved a balanced relationship with their family and with the larger society. Families that are exceptional in the centripetal period continue to balance several sets of developmental tasks at once. Furthermore, when a new child is born, a family that has moved into a more open position can close up, once again, to receive its newest member. If this centripetal force is very strong, there is a regression in the other children. Loss of developmental milestones in older siblings of newborns can be understood in the light of a general family tendency to be less differentiated and more internally responsive. If the family is deeply occupied with itself, the school-aged youngsters need support for their excursions outside the family from sources other than the parents, such as grandparents. If, however, the parents and the children have progressed in the family life cycle to a more differentiated stage, the system is unlikely to close so dramatically or to remain closed for long. Care of the infant may be assumed by someone other than a nuclear family member, such as a grandparent, babysitter, or child care center, so that the parents, as well as the other children, continue their involvements outside the home.

Divorce and remarriage represent the centrifugal and centripetal ends of the spectrum, respectively; therefore, they challenge a family system that is at the unfolding point of the "school-aged" era. Whether thoughtful and calm, or emotional and bitter, a divorce disrupts the balance between internal structure and external exploration. All family members are exposed prematurely to situations that may require resources outside the family for stabilization and support. For example, structure may be provided by court order, and support may be provided by counselors and mediators. Stability for children may be provided by grandparents, school personnel, or other concerned adults.

With remarriage, the family becomes more focused on itself, reversing the process of divorce, although the children of earlier marriages may or may not be involved in this turning inward. The greater consciousness of family and family roles, and the desire to establish family rituals and structures that occur when there is a remarriage result in a concentration on events within the family that is unusual in the families of most school-aged children. Alternatively, the remarried parents may not give much attention to the formation of a new family system with their new spouse; they may continue in the previous family life cycle with their own children, assuming that the new spouse will fit into that cycle.

The death of an immediate family member is painful and traumatic at any time in the life cycle. If the family member who died was old and had been ill, the death may be seen as a blessing and a relief, although the loss is still painful. Since death is a departure, a final differentiation of an individual from the family, this event is even more jarring for the family that is not at a centrifugal period in its life cycle. Therefore, although a death may be ''on time'' for the elderly individual, it may be ''off time'' for the family system.

Death also has the effect of bringing families together through funerals and mourning rituals; initial grieving is done in the company of other mourners. Like divorce and remarriage in the partially open family of the school-aged child, death can affect the family in such a way that the family becomes both more differentiating and more enclosing than usual. Since a death has a more pervasive effect on the entire family membership, however, there may not be alternative resources available within the family to stabilize the children. Siblings of children who have died often find themselves abandoned to the grief of their parents. These youngsters may have to seek structure outside the family. The family of a child who has died can become so wrapped up in the death that they appear to stand still, and the progress of the surviving children goes unobserved. These conditions may evolve one from the other, as the following case illustrates.

Debbie was 9 when her 3-year-old sister died of leukemia. Two younger brothers were 7 and 5. Debbie, as the oldest and a girl, was expected to care for herself and to help with the care of her brothers. Debbie's father immersed himself in his work and was rarely home. Her mother grieved openly and constantly. Debbie's schoolwork slipped, and she developed complaints that kept her out of school frequently. Her mother rarely protested her frequent excuses to stay home. The school did express concern and urged that she be evaluated. Services, including evaluation for Debbie and a support group for her bereaved parents, were available at the hospital where Debbie's sister had been treated. Both parents began to attend the group, and Debbie began to do better in school. Apparently, the bereaved parents group provided an opportunity for the parents to be companions in their grief so that Debbie could give more attention to her own tasks.

Two years later, when Debbie was 11, her mother brought her back for a reevaluation. Although she was attending school, her schoolwork was suffering again, and she often cut classes. At this time, she was dressed as if she were much more mature. She was wearing nailpolish, high-heeled shoes, a low-cut blouse, and a grown-up hairdo. She talked of boys and movie stars, expressing no interest in school at all. Her parents had continued to attend the parent group, and the child, apparently having turned to her own peers for support, had been drawn into a world demanding far more maturity than her years.

ASSESSMENT AND TREATMENT

Assessment of a family with young children requires an evaluation of the closeness of intrafamilial connections while the family is in the centripetal period and as the family emerges from it. Optimal family functioning in the centripetal period is not as differentiated and egalitarian as that of a family in the centrifugal period. In assessing a centripetal family, then, the strength of the attachment and bonding must be considered. How closely are the family members involved with each other and in family life? Are some family members excluded from the family cluster? What do these observations have to do with the problems experienced by the family?

When the children reach school age, too, there should be a clear hierarchy, set of rules, and imposition of values by adults on the children, even though these are subject to reevaluation and change throughout this period. With the family of school-aged children, relationships that are too close or too far apart could be related to problems. Are there structures, rules, and role expectations for family members, and are these honored? Is there freedom to move in and out of the family while attending to responsibilities as a family member? Is there accountability to the family in the context of exploration of other values and ideas?

Treatment of families with young children is intended to restore the family context to the degree of centripetal orientation appropriate for the care of its youngest members or to restore a balance in a complex family system that best accommodates the needs of all of its members. Some examples of assessment and treatment further illustrate the use of this model.

Families with Infants and Preschool Children

A family life cycle crisis in the centripetal period is usually manifested by symptomatology in an individual family member. Crises in families of newborns can affect either the parents or the infant. An illness, deformity, or prematurity of the infant interferes with bonding and attachment, as the infant and parents may be separated for an unusually long period. The infant may not respond to parents or may not stimulate them.

Colic in an otherwise healthy infant is a life crisis symptom. The colicky baby cannot be comforted, thwarting all the parents' attempts to make the world all right for it. This prevents the parents from developing the confidence in their knowledge of what the baby's needs are that characterizes the healthy parent-infant interaction. The parents of the colicky infant are exhausted, distraught, and irritable with each other as well as the baby. Who could blame the baby? Better to blame the adults who should be solving the problem. Focusing on each other's failures has a differentiating effect at a time when the family relationships should be less differentiated. Some pediatricians have favorite techniques for the treatment of colic, but the administration of these remedies in an irritable and quarrelsome family is unlikely to be soothing. Instead, sharing the care of the infant on a pre-established schedule so that each parent has time with the infant supported by the other parent's noninvolvement and each parent has time to rest may help to reduce the tension and to establish a kind of teamwork that will help the family function at a more coordinated and cohesive level.

Psychosis or depression in either of the parents is another kind of individual crisis associated with this period. These problems may occur when an individual is unable to cope with the shift in family environment and the demand for closeness, intimacy, and tolerance for boundary diffusion that are required at this time. In some cases, the fusion is too great, and the loss of boundaries is manifested in psychosis.

> Mrs. M was hospitalized for acute psychosis 3 weeks after the birth of her first child. Among many delusions was her conviction that she was an apple. This proved to be a preoccupation with her sense of having committed original sin, as when Adam and Eve ate the apple. She improved considerably with antipsychotic medication and even more rapidly when her son was brought to the hospital so that she could care for him with the support of the nurses. With the infant, her behavior alternated between detachment, as if she had forgotten about him, and an intense involvement in which she attributed to her son prescient thoughts such as "He's happy, now, because he knows his daddy is coming soon." On weekends, Mr. M joined his wife and baby in the hospital; in 3 more weeks, the family was discharged, considerably improved. This couple's own parents were too far away to visit. The hospital provided some "grandparent" support for them, with the outcome that the baby was more consistently cared for by both of his parents.

Desertion or alienation from the family in degrees varying from emotional unavailability to actual departure also cause crises in the centripetal period. Even as the children grow out of infancy and the family begins to unfold, the centripetal focus provides a more secure environment for the child.

> George was a 5-year-old adopted youngster. His father was a professional. His mother had juvenile diabetes with a number of sequelae, most recently including reduced vision with the threat of blindness. There was

a 10-year-old natural son. George was a cute, self-sufficient, and verbal youngster who had been adopted at the age of 3. His parents complained that he did not need them and that he "deliberately" did things to get attention, such as burn himself in the shower. They felt that he was on his way to becoming Al Capone.

The assessment revealed that family members were all occupied with personal things—the brother with school, the father with work, and the mother with her efforts to manage her condition and deny its seriousness. In short, they were not at all protective of George. The family was not sufficiently centripetal for his development.

Treatment included an emphasis on how young George was; for example, it was pointed out that he was too young to take showers by himself or to go to bed by himself. The parents were asked to observe George very carefully every day and to make sure that he was in a good mood, especially when he went to bed at night. They were instructed to help him with his self-care, because he was too young to do it himself, even though he might be able. After 2 weeks of this plan, the mother glowingly referred to George as "cute," and a major step had been taken toward adjusting the family environment.

Families of School-Aged Children

If the families of school-aged children are too centripetal or too centrifugal, characteristic problems can result. Elective mutism is a problem of school-aged children, and phobias in any family members can be quite characteristic of this period.

Ruth was 9 when she was referred for treatment of her elective mutism. Until that time, she had been treated by school personnel and her pediatrician without success. She lived with her handicapped mother, a retarded brother, and a sister with scoliosis. Another sister, 21, worked and also remained with the family. An older brother had left home, and no one knew his whereabouts. They did not talk about him anymore. Ruth was described as very talkative, in fact bossy, at home. The family was extremely closed and enmeshed. In the sessions, Ruth's mother and siblings had to interpret for her to the therapist. By their description, Ruth did the same for them at home.

Treatment was difficult. Ruth's mother was asked to spend time in Ruth's classroom every day in order to expand the family system to include Ruth's schooling. It was believed that, if Ruth's mother became a part of the school, then the school would be a part of the family. Ruth's mother not only had to overcome her embarrassment about her prosthetic leg and her lack of education, but also to see herself as a competent person who could work with some of the other children in the classroom. After several months of this program, Ruth began to speak a little to selected "outsiders" and later spoke in class.

The family in this period may have too much permeability and too little structure, producing precociously differentiated individuals and leading to characteristic problems. For example, the child who is unsupervised may become a delinquent, runaway, or vagrant, or the parent who abandons the family may turn to drugs or alcohol to replace the calming influence of the family.

Mrs. S had often fantasized about running away from the home where she lived with her husband and two boys, aged 5 and 8. Her older son was difficult, and she clashed with him more frequently as he approached 10 years old. He often threatened to run away himself. Mrs. S felt that she was stultified in her marriage, but did not recognize that her failure to provide adequate structure for her son contributed to her dissatisfaction. Finally, she did manage to leave, going for several months to another part of the United States. When she returned, she ambivalently sought to gain custody of the boys, even though she struggled continuously with them on their visits. When they were not with her, she pursued vague, uncommitted sexual relationships and began drinking.

Shortly after his divorce, Mr. S married a woman who was already established in a career, also a divorcee, but with no children. Together, they provided a clear if somewhat unimaginative structure for the boys. The first Mrs. S went to graduate school and, after graduating, secured a stable job and a steady relationship. Her drinking problem abated spontaneously at this point, through her own awareness of its destructiveness.

CONCLUSION

Families do adapt. If there is one parameter of health that seems to characterize families of all cultures and stages of the life cycle, it is flexibility or adaptability. As an old anatomy professor used to say, the way Mother Nature has designed the birth process, squeezing the infant down that narrow birth canal, it was a miracle that anyone survived! Likewise, the conditions for family life are never ideal, but most families survive. Therapists should study the families' own solutions to the complexity of their members' developmental needs before applying one from a therapeutic framework. Therapists working with families in the centripetal period are challenged by the ambiguity of family roles, the diffuseness of intrafamilial boundaries, and the often inexpressible emotional quality of interpersonal relationships. These states are often called "primitive," yet the model, here, indicates that individuals have the opportunity to go through such family cycles three times in their lifetime. In therapy with such families, metaphorical techniques, such as play, drawing, or enactments, are often more effective than talking. In the same vein, focusing on those moments of family life that are filled with the magic of intimacy—bedtime or times when cuddling and molding of individual into individual might take place—provides the most profound experience of connection for family members. Intimacy is the work of the family in this period, intimacy from which grows the individuation necessary for the next level of intimacy.

REFERENCES

Beavers, W.R. Healthy, midrange, and severely dysfunctional families. In F. Walsh (Ed.), *Normal family processes*. New York: Guilford, 1982.

Bergmann, A., Mahler, M., & Pine, F. *The psychological birth of the human infant*. New York: Basic Books, 1975.

Bowlby, J. *Attachment*. New York: Basic Books, 1969.

Friedman, E.H. Systems and ceremonies: A family view of rites of passage. In E.A.Carter & M. McGoldrick (Eds.), *The family life cycle*. New York: Gardner, 1980.

Greenberg, M., & Morris, N. Engrossment: The newborn's impact upon the father. *American Journal of Orthopsychiatry*, 1974, *44*(4), 520-531.

Haley, J. *Uncommon therapy*. Toronto: Norton, 1973.

Kennel, M., & Klaus, C. *Maternal-infant bonding*. St. Louis: CV Mosby, 1976.

Levinson, D.J., Darrow, C.N., Klein, E.B., Levinson, M.H., & McKee, B. *The seasons of a man's life*. New York: Knopf, 1978.

McGoldrick, M., & Carter, E.A. The family life cycle. In F. Walsh (Ed.), *Normal family processes*. New York: Guilford, 1982.

Robertson, J., & Robertson, J. *Young children in brief separation*. New York, New York University Film Library, 1967. (Film)

Sullivan, H.S. *The interpersonal theory of psychiatry*. New York: Norton, 1953.

Walsh, F. The family in later life. In E.A. Carter & M. McGoldrick (Eds.), *The family life cycle*. New York: Gardner, 1980.

4. Learning a Systems Orientation from Parents

W. Robert Beavers, MD
Clinical Professor of Psychiatry
University of Texas Health Science Center
Executive Director
Southwest Family Institute
Dallas, Texas

FAMILIES, LIKE INDIVIDUALS, HAVE A KIND OF "SCRIPT"; THEY HAVE A beginning and a developmental course, although the end is always in question. Are Darwin's ideas dead? Does any family totally disappear?

In former times, physicians of the mind tracked the life history of their patients. Neurologists and alienists were intensely, sometimes feverishly, interested in the natural history of mental disease. They did not expect themselves to do anything particularly remarkable—their expertise lay in *knowing* the multiple and subtle evidences of syndromes. Freud was to these spectator experts something of a spoilsport because he tried to intervene, to change things, to transmute neurotic illness into common unhappiness. He became a highly visible missionary to the mind. By today's standards, however, his therapy seems slow and cautious. With ever more driven and desperate optimism, legions of mental health professionals have pursued active interventionist techniques.

These two approaches to emotional problems or disease, a data-gathering, educational (anthropological) approach and an energetic, fix-it (missionary) approach, have alternated in prominence in the mental health field for close to 100 years. Each has been associated with power and abuse. In the 1920s, for example, when the autointoxication theory of madness was widely accepted, the colons of suffering schizophrenics were removed in an effort to cure their illness. The results, when dispassionately evaluated, were psychotic people with no colons, a pitiful failure of the missionary "intervention" (Davis, 1960). In the last 70 years or so, the Freudian missionary approach has been attenuated so that it has become much closer to the anthropological approach—observe, record, comment, and report. On the other hand, with some disorders (e.g., anorexia nervosa), there is considerable evidence that active therapeutic intervention is much more effective than a reflective stance (Minuchin, Rosuan, & Baker, 1978).

The psychotherapist of the late 20th century is inevitably dealing with the tension of these polar positions. There are simultaneous directives to be active and to be passive, to fix it and to understand it. The dual themes are found in psychoanalytic arguments, such as Kohut (1977), with his emphasis on the need for real human interchange in treatment, versus orthodox Freudians who still emphasize the nonreal or transference issues; in family therapy, usually a more active orientation, versus individual therapy; and in various other schools of psychotherapy, such as Haley's (1977) belief in the therapist's responsibility for family change versus Boszormenyi-Nagy's (1981) focus on each family member's responsibility.

At a different level, family members have the same dilemma. Is there a quick fix for emotional pain, prepackaged and bought off the shelf? Or, is it necessary to know one's family history, the ethnic and cultural roots, and the ways in which the style and tempo of the present family are tied to past generations of family systems, beliefs, and attitudes? This dilemma is highly significant, yet it is not always defined by therapists or patients. In the powerful interchange between family and therapist, health or normality may be defined according to a particular style, or the complex history and patterns of both the husband's family and the wife's family may be utilized to determine the best way to succeed in family developmental tasks.

Intervention with couples is sometimes quite active and sometimes reflective; sometimes intervention takes the form of a partnership between couple and therapist. The couple should be encouraged to develop the anthropological approach to their families of origin and to avoid being missionaries to them. An activist approach to the family of origin has been well delineated ("Toward the Differentiation of a Self," 1972). Couples can develop a systems orientation by learning the rules, processes, and patterns of their families of origin and utilizing this information to establish the current family identity. Choices are made: this to keep, this to modify, this to avoid. There is no attempt to change the family of origin except by example or in response to a request for help, however. The result of this analysis is an elevated awareness of previously unnoticed family processes. Greater awareness increases the number of available choices, and a wider range of choices increases negotiating possibilities.

METHODS USED IN THE SYSTEMS APPROACH

There are probably an infinite number of ways for the anthropological systems approach to be taught and learned. The following are commonly used methods:

- eyewitness accounts: verbal descriptions of the family of origin, with free-for-all kibitzing by spouses and/or children
- field trips: visits to the family of origin with the directed goal of studying together, observing, and finding time to compare notes
- inviting the natives to tea: visits from the family of origin and observation of their interactions with each other and with the current family
- case studies: invitations to parents or siblings of the couple involved in treatment to attend a session

- data analysis: integration of the various ways of observing how families interact and sharing of conclusions about goals, processes, and rules for the present family

Eyewitness Accounts

Even in the first interview, there is usually an opportunity to ask each spouse how his or her growing up experience influences present behavior. If one partner falters, the other eagerly offers suggestions.

Sue and Don T, aged 32 and 33, had come to a children's clinic because of their 7-year-old son's behavior problem, but they soon agreed that their marriage was a bigger problem. Sue thought she wanted a divorce, as she found Don sexually uninteresting, emotionally distant, and intolerably sloppy. Don, in turn, spoke of his desire to continue the marriage, even though his wife seemed to him constantly depressed, driven, unresponsive, and joyless. In the couple's first interview, Don volunteered that his distancing was related to his family experience; both his mother and his father drank heavily and frequently were physically abusive to each other, to him, and to his siblings. Sue recalled that her parents also drank heavily. There was no physical abuse in her family, but there were tremendous efforts to control the family's day-to-day activities. Meals were exactly at 6:00, everything was tidy, and there were devastating verbal attacks on anyone who faltered.

Sue remembered liking Don originally because he was comfortable to be around and made her feel more confident in social situations. He recalled that she helped him become more stable and responsible, although this was a gradual process over several years.

Rather quickly, several things became apparent to the couple and the therapist. Each spouse had initially described all the marital faults of the other. As they began to talk of their upbringing, however, each could more easily admit to some long-standing difficulties and maladaptive behavior that contributed to their dreary marriage. Already, the awareness of a systems orientation was dawning. From "The problem is you," the discussion went to "The problem is ours" and "We each missed something growing up." Furthermore, they began to see that people usually want to divorce for the same reasons that they wanted to marry. In this instance, Sue loved Don partly because of his "laid back" attitude, which made her feel accepted, and yet she criticized him because he was not more structured. Don, on the other hand, loved Sue partly because of her ability to make him want to be responsible, but he was frustrated and angry at her criticism of his sloppy ways and her lack of desire to have fun.

With more therapy, each could see that their families of origin had some strengths, values, and traditions that were worthy of respect. Sue's parents were responsible even under stress; Don's parents gave their children latitude and freedom.

In the process of discussing these three families, the present one and that of each spouse, the familiar victim-persecutor-rescuer triad was abandoned and replaced with an appreciation for mixed feelings, mixed virtues, and mixed evils. Sue and Don were able to move from the judgmental to the evaluative in remembering and observing their families. Inevitably, they softened the judgmental aspects of their attitudes toward each other, trying to understand rather than futilely attempting to change each other. From this more open approach, negotiation was more successful, and change did occur.

Field Trips

Every married couple develops family rules and patterns that are, inevitably, different from those of either spouse's family. These rules and patterns may be unclear and undefined, or they may be relatively clear or even explicit as a result of discussion and negotiation (Beavers, 1982). Rules may be a continuing source of marital conflict, or, when both spouses believe they have improved on the rules of their own families, the rules can be a source of pride and cohesiveness. Particularly when one or both partners have been in treatment, these grown children may become uninvited missionaries, making repeated attempts to change their parents' way of operating and thus bring "enlightenment" to a family that has been functioning for 25 years or more. The results of this missionary approach are uniformly poor. When the family visits the family of origin of one spouse, conflicts between generations are intensified, not resolved. Hurt feelings multiply, and the visit becomes a nightmare.

When a couple is planning a parental visit, the therapist should call attention to the defects of the missionary approach and should emphasize the value and relative ease of an anthropological orientation. Here is an opportunity to learn at first hand the rules of one partner's family of origin. If it is believed, for example, that Mother is terribly dominating, how does Mother dominate, and what does Father do when she makes her moves? What does Mother obtain for herself in this habitual pattern? What are the advantages to Father? If there are children from the family of origin still in the home, how does each child interact in the parents' predictable "dance"?

An impressive amount of data can be obtained in a short time with this approach. The couple learns that control is reciprocal—loud talking is countered with silence, intimidation is defeated by helplessness, and needs are met in unexpected ways. Even with their strange customs, the natives have managed to survive for many years, and the observer who does not judge too quickly will develop respect for these survival strategies.

The couple should take care that neither is "cut from the pack" during the visit. It is perilous to go into a strange culture alone: one either "goes native" or is seen as quite weird. The couple needs to arrange time alone together in order to talk about what they have learned, to regroup, and to get back together so that the learning can continue.

The spouse whose family is being visited understandably tends to fall back into the role dictated in years past. (In fact, this may be the principal reason for the missionary approach; the fear of regression can produce the intense effort to convert.) Such a tendency, if predicted and expected, can be successfully avoided by frequently reconnecting with the spouse not so ingrained with the family history.

Mr. and Mrs. H came into treatment because their 11-year-old daughter's behavior had become a problem at school and at home. Mr. H came from a family that was honest, upright, and conventional, as was Mr. H. Mrs. H, in contrast, had had a painful early life. Her mother and father were divorced when she was 10; her stepfather, who entered the picture when she was 12, had sexually molested Mrs. H from the time she was 12 until she left home at the age of 17. She was never able to make her mother believe that the stepfather was abusing her. Mr. and Mrs. H agreed that his family was great and hers was lousy.

A visit to his family was planned, and the anthropological approach was recommended. After the week's visit, Mr. H commented that his family might be virtuous, but it sure was *dull*. Everything was so controlled, so predictable. He noted that each person in his family seemed to dampen any spontaneity in the others, and he was newly appreciative of his wife's vivacity and occasional unpredictability. The next step was to arrange for a visit with Mrs. H's mother and stepfather to see how this family could have produced a woman as delightful and interesting as Mrs. H. Following this visit, Mr. and Mrs. H were asked to make a list of the factors noticed in her family that were different from those in his but seemed to have contributed to Mrs. H's strengths.

In this way, their own destructive mythology was successfully challenged; Mrs. H held her head higher and stopped ruminating about her bad stepfather. The troubling black and white picture of "back street girl" and "white knight," which had contributed to so much covert conflict, was transformed into a multicolored picture of frequently spontaneous spouses, who approached joint decision making from an equal position.

In the process, the daughter's difficulties faded into insignificance, since she was no longer carrying the burden of the family conflict.

Visiting both families became more fun. Mrs. H really tried to understand why her mother had stayed with the stepfather, seemingly oblivious to Mrs. H's problems with the stepfather's sexual advances. She could empathize with the plight of a divorced woman with three children and no job skills. She observed that adaptability may sometimes include behavior that is not "by the book"—at least not by an etiquette book. This, in turn, helped her forgive herself for the pleasure she had experienced in the sexual molestation; she had felt not only disgust, fear, apprehension, and anger, but also pleasure. This was a secret she kept even from herself until she understood and forgave her mother. In the process, her adamant hatred of her stepfather abated.

Some parents can rain judgmental fire and brimstone down on their married offspring. Criticism may involve the marriage or spouse of the offspring, or it may concern the grandchildren and the way they are being raised. Buckling under attacks such as these by taking on the rules of the tribe and giving up one's own is the risk of "going native." There are tools that can be used to avoid this kind of regression or loss of identity: (1) staying in touch with each other, (2) avoiding triangles, (3) taking time-outs, (4) declaring oneself, and (5) asking questions.

Staying in Touch with Each Other

The current family's rules are most likely to be preserved when couples are attuned to each other. While visiting their grandparents, children will shamelessly use Grandma or Grandpa as a lever to get a short-term advantage. Grandma or Grandpa may equally shamelessly circumvent their child (the parent) regarding diets, sleep patterns, and the like. It is only as couples work together that they can maintain the fabric of their personal and family identity. Attacks from parents regarding the choice of a spouse, child-rearing techniques, lovability, or loyalty can best be resisted with the support of a dependable partner. When single parents visit their own parents, it may be wise to take a friend, spend time with a good friend in the town or city visited, or to make very short visits. All alone, it is difficult to resist the power of another family system for long.

Avoiding Triangles

Families of origin may have rules that include regular triangulation. One part of the triangle may be buffeted from both sides, or, conversely, one side may manipulate the other two sides by keeping them apart. Couples should watch for such triangulations in an anthropological manner, but should never take action when others—not the couple—are involved. Many families survive quite well with techniques that offend systems sophisticates, and changing them would require two things that are missing—motivation from the family members and motivation from the child-become-adult to handle all the repercussions that inevitably occur with growth-oriented changes.

It is necessary for the couple to avoid triangles whenever they are identified, however. Does Dad get daughter off in the corner and complain about Mother? Does Mom get son-in-law in the kitchen and subtly suggest that he must have to put up with a great deal? The spouse involved should back out, rejoin the group, cry for spouse, or get a coughing fit, whatever is required to resolve the situation. Practice time in treatment sessions makes this tool useful. The playing back and forth of identifying triangles and blocking them in the present family and in the family of origin further sharpens systems skills and encourages the high morale associated with successful teams.

Taking Time-outs

A family's successful visit to one parent's family of origin requires time to withdraw, to regroup, to share perceptions, and to redefine family boundaries. A parent in one family is a child in the other; the time-out allows that individual to maintain or reinstitute the sense of being an adult and having a partner, not a parent. Taking walks, going to a movie, visiting friends, and letting the grandparents take the children on outings while the couple stays home are all simple and practical ways to maintain present family rules.

Declaring Oneself

Being clear about choices, risks, and needs need not be confused with being judgmental or tyrannically imposing one family's rules on another.

> Mr. and Mrs. T had been in treatment as a couple and, intermittently, as a family with their two daughters, aged 8 and 10, for about 6 months, primarily because of marital conflict and occasional concern with one or the other daughter's behavior. Mrs. T stated that she had attempted, during the early years of the marriage, to be whatever her husband desired. In the last 3 years, however, she had been angry and depressed, groping for some identity separate from that of her husband. Mr. T agreed with this summary, but stated that he had trouble either expressing or accepting anger and was not at all sure how to deal with Mrs. T.

Mrs. T's father had died some years previously, and her mother had remarried. Mrs. T had always felt that her father understood and supported her, but she and her mother had always clashed. Her mother was perceived as insensitive, dominating, and demanding, producing in Mrs. T alternating rage and guilt.

The family planned a week's visit to their home state, which entailed a visit to Mrs. T's mother and stepfather. The therapist discussed in detail the approach and tools previously described. A special concern involved where the family would stay. On previous trips, Mrs. T's mother had insisted on their staying at her house; this time Mrs. T wanted to stay in a nearby motel, so she could have some breathing room. The therapist and Mr. T supported her in this desire, and the T family did indeed stay in a motel during the visit. Mrs. T's mother was terribly "hurt"; she suggested that her daughter did not love her. This was an effort at intimidation, but it was to no avail. Mrs. T did not get hysterical and did not lash out, as was her previous pattern. She simply stated her wish and, with her husband's help, followed through effectively.

This event produced several significant changes. Mrs. T was much less childlike—being neither compliant nor rebellious, but rather more definite and clear, with her mother, stepfather, husband, and therapist. Mrs. T's mother reportedly began to talk to her as an adult and to show some consideration for her opinions and wishes.

Asking Questions

Another method of resisting moralistic attacks and refusing to accept guilt is to ask questions. This is a time-honored maneuver of therapists that should be shared with patients. When parents are criticizing their offspring's child-rearing practices, for example, a careful investigation of their perceptions and alternative plan of action usually keeps the situation under control. If the attack is accompanied by clear advice (e.g., "You need to make that child continue her music lessons "), questions can be asked regarding when the speaker has used the technique, with whom, and what were the results. Such inquiries usually dilute unpleasant either/or situations into (at worst) tedious discussion. Occasionally, they provide an opportunity for real help.

Inviting the Natives to Tea

A visit from one of the spouse's parents (or whole family, for that matter) makes it possible to extend the anthropological approach to include probes. Family therapists use probes routinely to determine the family's adaptive capacity, characteristic patterns, and response to novelty. With coaching, the family in treatment can do just as well with probes. The key to the success of this additional tool is its use in the couple's own home. For example, several couples have found that the sternly nondrinking parents of one spouse accepted easily and without question the couple's offering choices of before dinner beverages that include cocktails. The same parents would have been outraged had the couples brought liquor with them on a visit, and many of the couples had been convinced that Mom and Dad would self-destruct, commit mayhem, or do some other dire or unclear thing if presented with any other family pattern. It is not possible to determine the degree of family adaptability, however, until the family is presented with the untried.

> Mr. and Mrs. Q had been married several years before they had a child. In the midst of their joy over their new baby, John, they learned that he had a rare metabolic disturbance that could impair his intellectual and emotional development. They subsequently had an unblemished child, Sophie, but they were frequently preoccupied with John's development and adjustment problems; they necessarily consulted many medical and mental health experts. Whenever they visited Mrs. Q's parents, who lived in the same city, the parenting program that had been carefully worked out for John with these various professionals was effectively destroyed. Mrs. Q's father and mother would offer John anything he wanted and would almost ignore Sophie.
>
> The therapist coached Mr. and Mrs. Q in making very short, only 1- and 2-hour visits to her parents. Using the children (especially John) as "bait," Mr. and Mrs. Q invited Mrs. Q's parents to the Q home, where they could insist on conformity to the family rules. The grandparents were invited to assist Mr. and Mrs. Q in helping John do well, with the method clearly outlined. The grandparents accepted the family rules, and soon longer visits could be made to the grandparents when it was desired by all concerned.
>
> This exercise not only provided a fine opportunity for Mr. and Mrs. Q together to learn many systems concepts and strategies, but also allowed them to be closer rather than alienated from her parents.

Case Studies

In many cases, families of origin live elsewhere and cannot participate regularly in treatment sessions, even if it were deemed valuable. Their occasional visits are always educational, usually enjoyable, and sometimes pivotal in inducing useful change, however.

> Mr. and Mrs. T, mentioned earlier, invited Mrs. T's mother into the sessions. Whereas before, Mrs. T had merely reported her interaction with her mother, she now had an opportunity to live it in the company of the therapist. Somehow in this setting, she found it easier to view her mother as quite anxious, doubtful of her own lovability, and desperately masking these unpleasant feelings by intermittent attacks on her daughter. Mrs. T could even identify some of her mother's behavior in herself; since she was no longer so certain that this behavior was malevolent, Mrs. T was able to forgive herself as well as her mother.

> Mr. and Mrs. J were locked in a well-bred, but endless, struggle for control and frequently forgot to look for any pleasure in each other, in life, or in their children. A frequent approach in such intense battles is to ask at strategic times, "What are you trying to do? *Right now,* what are you trying to do and how are you trying to do it?" This usually shifts the focus to gratification, rather than control, and negotiation proceeds.
>
> In the case of Mr. and Mrs. J, however, unexpected help arrived. Mr. J asked his parents to participate in the session while they were visiting from another state, more because of the parents' curiosity than because of any current problem. In the course of the interview, Mr. J's mother told how Mr. J had become anorectic at the age of 5, soon after the death of his brother. The account of these events, which had been totally repressed by Mr. J, provided for everyone a sharply increased awareness of the emotional hunger, denial, loss, and efforts at control that had influenced the couple's relationship patterns.

Data Analysis

During treatment, these various ways of understanding family functions and processes can be integrated, and shared conclusions can be reached. A systems orientation develops. Healthy families have a systems orientation; they generally understand that the causes of problems are multiple, and that causes and effects are usually interchangeable. People can almost always influence others, but they are never omnipotent (Beavers, 1977). In addition, there are characteristic systems qualities in healthy family interaction related to boundaries, power, differentiation, choices, ambivalence, conflict resolution, and the like (Beavers, 1976; Beavers, 1981; Beavers & Kaslow, 1981).

CONCLUSION

A family of origin can be a powerful force in the efforts of therapists and families to understand family processes and to increase the skills, enjoyment, and competence of family members in treatment. The approach is not a quick fix to family difficulties, although it often can be used to resolve long-standing family fights. Family theorists, family therapists, and family members are all engaged in similar activities, with a similar classical dilemma. The anthropological approach to families involves learning how people get together and meet basic needs, with little emphasis on the "right" way to do it. In this fashion, patients and therapists become students of systems, ever ready to negotiate novel solutions to familiar problems.

REFERENCES

Beavers, W.R. A theoretical basis for family evaluation. In J.M. Lewis, W.R. Beavers, J.T. Gossett, & V.A. Phillips (Eds.), *No single thread: Psychological health in family systems*. New York: Brunner/Mazel, 1976.

Beavers, W.R. *Psychotherapy and growth: A family systems perspective*. New York: Brunner/Mazel, 1977.

Beavers, W.R. A systems model of family for family therapists. *Journal of Marital and Family Therapy*, 1981, 7(3), 299-307.

Beavers, W.R. Healthy, midrange and severely dysfunctional families. In F. Walsh (Ed.), *Normal family processes*. New York: Guilford Press, 1982.

Beavers, W.R., & Kaslow, F.W. The anatomy of hope. *Journal of Marital and Family Therapy*, 1981, 7(2), 119-126.

Boszormenyi-Nagy, I. Contextual therapy: Therapeutic leverages in mobilizing trust. In R.J. Green & J.L. Framo (Eds.), *Family therapy: Major contributions*. New York: International Universities Press, 1981.

Davis, F.H. Patterns in the distortion of scientific method. *Southern Medical Journal*, 1960, 53, 1117.

Haley, J. *Problem solving therapy*. San Francisco: Jossey-Bass, 1977.

Kohut, H. *The restoration of the self*. New York: International Universities Press, 1977.

Minuchin, S., Rosman, B.C., & Baker, L. *Psychosomatic families: Anorexia nervosa in context*. Cambridge, MA: Harvard University Press, 1978.

Toward the differentiation of a self in one's own family. In J.L. Framo (Ed.), *Family interaction: A dialogue between family researchers and family therapists*. New York: Springer, 1972.

5. Coming of Age in the Fourth Decade

Donald S. Williamson, PhD
Houston Family Institute
Houston, Texas

Psychotherapeutic consultation may itself present the ultimate example of the "solution becoming the problem" (Watzlawick,
Weakland, & Fisch, 1974). Clients come to therapy because they are unable
to adopt a responsible adult posture in life, in the social world in general, and
in the family of origin in particular. Ironically, traditional one-to-one
psychotherapy is likely to place the already overly dependent client into an
even more dependent position in order to be "done unto" and helped. This
routinely confirms the personal inadequacy that is usually the client's
problem in the first place. It is therefore particularly important that the
consultation experience offer the client a context in which to establish
personal authority and that it should affirm rather than undercut this authority. Paradoxically, then, one goal of consultation is to provide an opportunity
for the client to acknowledge that help cannot come from outside the self.

Therapists cannot transcend their own lives to the extent that they can
analyze a client's life from any objective position. This is particularly true in
the context of family therapy, since family therapists are constantly at risk of
being inducted by the family. This emphasis on the personal authority and
responsibility of the client for his or her own life, behavior, and destiny, is
the essential character of the method of intergenerational family therapy
developed by this writer (Williamson, 1981, 1982a, 1982b, 1983).

Because of mutual intimidation, the members of both the first and the
second generations collude in order to avoid facing and renegotiating
intergenerational politics. This collusion maintains the denial of aging and
death, which reduces anxiety for both generations. The collusion may even
include the therapist, since it also enables the therapist to avoid anxiety
about aging and dying. This intimidation may be seen as the psychological
opposite of personal freedom. As a result of this reciprocal, intergenerational intimidation and denial, adults in the second generation may be caught
between an involuntary, learned fusion with and protection of the older
parents on the one hand, and a conscious distaste for and distancing from
them on the other. This is very widespread and is simultaneously an
intrapsychic and a systemic phenomenon. It is the source of a host of social-
psychological problems in all three generations, as well as in the political
organization in the three-generation family.

Successful renegotiation of intergenerational politics via the termination
of the intergenerational hierarchical boundary is known as the achievement
of personal authority in the family system (Williamson, 1982b). In essence,
this means the establishment of peerhood with former parents. Individuation
is normally viewed as the psychological, if not the logical, opposite of
fusion-triangulation (Bowen, 1974). Intimacy can be conceptualized as

voluntary fusion, that is, fusion that can be entered into (or not entered into) or terminated more or less at will. Personal authority in the family system is therefore a synthesizing construct between individuation and intimacy; it is individuation plus, or coexisting with, intimacy.

BASIC ASSUMPTIONS

Their personal health and well-being require that adults be able to live with a clear sense of connection to, as well as belongingness and intimacy with, the members of the previous generation, particularly the parents who are their biopsychosocial source. This is true whether the parents are deceased or alive. The termination of transgenerational mortgage payments and the acquisition of clear and clean title to one's own life and destiny is the dominating developmental issue of adult life. But how does one pay off the indebtedness, both real and imaginary, and take full personal responsibility for oneself? In other words, how does one synchromesh individuation with intimacy within the interactional patterns in the family of origin, and consequently in one's own marriage and nuclear family?

Resolution of this question requires a renegotiation of the intergenerational hierarchical boundary, leading to the achievement of peerhood with former parents. Some family-of-origin theorists believe that change is achieved only very slowly and that its outcome is modest at best (Boszormenyi-Nagy & Ulrich, 1981; Kerr, 1981). These and other pessimistic positions may be due to the fact that these therapeutic viewpoints do not deal directly with the source of power, which is the parents and the parental power coalition of the previous generation. The differentiation of self (Bowen, 1972), the achievement of relational ethics in the family (Boszormenyi-Nagy, 1981), the resolution of unmourned loss experiences (Paul & Grosser, 1965), or the refurbishing of distorted parental introjects (Framo, 1976), all require radical intergenerational restructuring. In this regard, the concept of personal authority in the family system may be seen as brief transgenerational family therapy that goes right to the political jugular—the power position necessarily and properly inherent in the role of parent and in the parental power coalition. This kind of radical political change permits a pattern of coexistence and synchromeshing of individuation with intimacy.

Personal authority in the family system is a form of family-of-origin consultation that is both psychodynamic and systemic in character. It is indeed an intervention into the self-system of the client, yet it clearly works with the self-system in the context of the family system, including both the

amily of origin and the nuclear family. Therefore, in contrast to differentia-
ion of self within the family of origin, this approach results in a fully
eciprocal, interactional, intergenerational event.

Termination of the intergenerational hierarchical boundary can be seen as
a continuous developmental process that occurs over a period of 10 to 15
years. At the same time, it is possible to highlight the discontinuous,
historical moment in time sequences, in which the adult client establishes
peerhood with parents, says goodbye to "Mommy" and "Daddy," and
openly terminates the underlying romantic involvement with the opposite
sex parent. These sequences are conscious, explicit, willful, scheduled,
and, above all, face to face.

The consultation experience is characterized by humor and playfulness,
with much use of paradox and absurdity (Williamson, 1982b). It is assumed
that there is an inherent absurdity in all intimate behavior, beginning most
delightfully with the mythology of romance. The consultation method has
two core premises: (1) the client comes to get help to restrain change, that is,
to change very slowly; (2) all change is from within, so the help to be
received is an awareness that there is no help to be found outside of the self.

Intergenerational political renegotiation is fundamentally reciprocal. It is
freeing and unburdening, which is to say differentiating, for both generations. To begin with, the intergenerational intimidation is reciprocal. Parents are intimidated by their children because the second generation
represents a walking judgment, indictment, and evaluation of the parents'
parenting and, therefore, of the parents themselves. When the timing is good
and the reciprocity is well balanced, both generations feel relieved and
unburdened by the change. Parents no longer feel guilty and responsible for
the progress, success, and happiness of "former children." They can be
more relaxed and live with less regret and less guilt regarding the present
welfare and future achievement of the next generation. There is now a
reciprocal compassion in each generation for the humanness and finiteness
of the other. The unburdening of the first generation reinforces the political
initiative toward peerhood taken by the second generation, and the cycle (or
better, the circle) continues ever more swiftly.

Another basic assumption of this therapeutic orientation is that "the
future lies ahead" rather than behind. By the very act of acknowledging that
the past cannot be changed or denied, the client changes his or her own past.
For what needs to be changed is not "the facts" of the past, but the
continuing demand that it be different. Since nothing is subject to therapeutic intervention unless it is emotionally real and immediately present in the
room, there is only present reality available in the consultation. This present

reality (of *past* events), is changed as it is reframed by the client, giving a more useful meaning to happenings that are still emotionally present, although related chronologically to past events.

The bottom line of this kind of family-of-origin consultation is the identification, acknowledgment, and, most critically, the acceptance of one's parents exactly as they are. This is in contrast to the earlier reciprocal demand by each generation (taught to the second by the first—who, of course, learned it from the first when they were the second) that the other should somehow be different, or better, or more, or less of something. This new resolution includes the termination of the primary love affair with the opposite sex parent and the ending of the primitive romantic dream. There is an accompanying acknowledgment to the self, however, that the self is free to be different even though the parent remains the same. To be able to accept the parents exactly as they are, while simultaneously declaring the different-ness of the self, is the essence of personal authority in the family system and is an important, perhaps the most important, basis for truth in personal living.

The small group of four members is the staging ground, the context in which the adult prepares to go "on stage" with the parents (Williamson, 1982b). The small group becomes a Greek chorus to the consultant and then to each other, gradually sharing and participating fully in the consultant role. Small group consultation is first and foremost good theater. No one can be rushed. Each person needs to say all of his or her own lines and to move at his or her own rhythm. Occasionally, a group of like-minded and trans-ference-prone siblings may form a negative coalition against the consultant-parent. For this and other reasons, the selection of the small group requires a high level of discrimination to ensure that the small group offers support, confrontation, competition, and modeling. The fundamental underlying premise is: Isn't it time to remove the parenting burden from our parents? This is exhilarating for the group members, even as it is scary to contem-plate.

THE CONSULTATION PROCESS

The initial experience of moving away from the family of origin emo-tionally and reducing an overinvolved physical and social contact with parents is viewed as prechange change, or preparatory change. By talking to siblings and other members of the extended family and making tapes of imaginary conversations with each parent, clients can reduce their emotionality within the family of origin. They can also identify important agenda items for the face-to-face conversations that lie ahead.

At the beginning, parents are understandably reluctant to share their inner life process and experience with their former children, since they expect even adult children to continue to behave in the punishing and exploitative manner characteristic of young children. As parents realize that the second generation is beginning to think, feel, and behave as adults in relationship to them, however, each parent comes to trust son or daughter enough to be able to talk openly about the spouse and the parental marriage without feeling disloyal for criticizing the spouse "in front of the children." Also, the adult in the second generation is now able to hear this more honest feedback without fusion or triangulation and without losing respect for the other parent. Adult children can now respond with compassion without forfeiting their own positions (Bowen, 1978).

The same sex parent remains the most important person of that sex in the client's life "forever." In contrast, the position of the opposite sex parent must be renegotiated in favor of the client's spouse. This requires a major shift in personal loyalties that is not easy to achieve. For many people, loyalties move back and forth, depending on the context of the moment and the physical proximity of the members of the family of origin.

The client goes through certain chronological sequences in the consultation process. First, the more intense feelings in the transgenerational affective heritage are resolved. The consultant group hears and accepts empathically the rage, bewilderment, and grief of the member concerning the past, but soon goes on to suggest that the past might have been in fact quite different than the client remembers it was. The client then begins to participate in reframing his own history. Second, the emotional sting is pulled from these matters through the preparation. They are subsequently discussed between the adult client and parents so that the client has an opportunity for interaction around these previously high stakes matters as an *adult* and the past can be closed. Redress as this is normally understood is neither possible nor necessary. Third, the client pursues and discovers the real inner life experience of the parents, which makes it possible to explore lacunae, secrets, skeletons, and unmourned losses transmitted across the generations. Many people have unconsciously and spontaneously reframed their own historical experiences in order to avoid facing the implications. The consultation deliberately sabotages these denials so that the client can learn to express rejected aspects of himself in verbal symbols and so assimilate these into the self-system. For a period of time, however, the client feels much worse than he did originally.

The client is now in a position to withdraw from a triangulated role within the parental marriage. This is a key aspect of the experience of renegotiating transgenerational loyalties and legacies. The client soon develops new loyalties, first to the consultation process, then to himself. He gives up the romantic connection to the opposite sex parent during the face-to-face transactions. The client then declares his personal differentness directly in conversation with the parents. Acknowledgment of this differentness of the self in the context of acceptance of the parent's sameness is the essence of personal authority in the family system. This ambiance of mutual compassion and forgiveness allows even more space for differentness.

Finally, there is a mutual acknowledgment of the aging and approaching death of the parents, with its unavoidable implication of the approaching death of the client. In this conversation, the client has a chance to evaluate both the extent and the ways in which each parent has achieved integrity or despair in life (Erikson, 1959). At this time, the consultant can gently point out to the client the parent's vulnerability that the client cannot see. This awareness relieves intimidation, idealism, rage, or dependency. For example, when a client asks the parent about approaching death, the parent may reply, "Why, I never give it a thought . . . it doesn't bother me." The consultant may comment quietly to the client, "You can see the terror." This is the valuable kind of experience that enables the adult (in the second generation) to give up intimidation, recognize the frailty of the formerly powerful parent, and embrace the parent with compassion and acceptance.

SPECIAL PROBLEMS

A number of clinical situations create special problems for the adult seeking personal authority in the family system. For some parents, the loss of the structural parental position and accompanying political power is very threatening to their self-identity and self-esteem; the loss may provoke considerable anger. The loss of position is a powerful reminder of death's imminence, and produces sadness and grief at the anticipation of this ultimate loss. This occasion calls for massive support to parents from the consultant. To complicate matters, the client may be experiencing a sense of exhilaration at recovering a new piece of self from the previous generation, at the same time the parents are experiencing this sense of loss. Special handling and care are required when the internalized role as parent appears structurally necessary to the present psychological orientation and self-definition of a parent.

A marital partner who participates alone in a family-of-origin small group will probably move in the direction of individuation and personal autonomy. Even when the spouse is interested and supportive, this move has an unpredictable, not necessarily supportive, impact on the relationship. By contrast, marital therapy may unwittingly support the fusion in a marriage by making it difficult for either partner to initiate any differentiation. Furthermore, it may immobilize initiative by, for example, repeatedly demonstrating the circularity and reciprocity in the behavioral patterns of the marital relationship.

Where the dominating bond in a marriage has developed via the re-creation of each partner's parents' marriage or each partner's relationship to the opposite sex parent, the resolution available through family-of-origin therapy may remove much of the unconscious, but connecting, emotional cement in the present marriage. This is likely to produce marital crisis. Not infrequently, someone comes for consultation in order to find the resources to move away from a highly dysfunctional marriage or a scapegoat position within that marriage. This may be the client's intention, regardless of the spouse's level of readiness for change. Traditional one-to-one psychotherapy has often been detrimental to the marriage of the individual client, perhaps because this type of therapy tends to provide substitute relational support for the one who is in treatment. (Similarly, conjoint marital therapy, in its even-handedness, may support continuing fusion.) Thus, given an insensitivity to the marriage of someone participating in a family-of-origin group, the therapy may take on a character reminiscent of individual psychotherapy in its implicit threat to the stability of the client's marriage.

The client's marriage is especially vulnerable when the client has been held in the marriage, at least partly, by anxiety about personal identity, lovability, and loneliness or by an identification of the spouse with the opposite sex parent, which re-creates for the client a scapegoated parental role from the family of origin. When the client begins to move out of these positions, it may be difficult to renegotiate the politics of the marriage unless both partners are somehow involved in the change process from its inception. This is particularly so if a spouse has been exploited, or physically or emotionally abused within the marriage for any sustained period of time. Finally, a client who is now able to give up a dependent connection to parents through the family-of-origin consultation, but whose marriage is not presently being experienced as nurturing, may subsequently feel hungry for caring and supporting relationships apart from the marriage.

At all times, therefore, it is essential to be aware of the marital process of each member of the small group in intergenerational consultation. The interested and calling spouse should be seen only with the marital partner for the first screening interview(s). This ensures that the nonworking partner is knowledgeable about and at the very least neutral toward the work of the spouse. The consultant should explain that any group member's spouse may attend the sessions as an observer at any time and that the nonworking spouse can request a conjoint interview if ever concerned. Finally, the consultant should schedule a conjoint interview whenever he or she perceives any distress about the present trends in a client's marriage. In short, the consultant adopts an attitude of "multidirectional partiality" toward the extended family of each group member, with particular sensitivity to the absent spouse. Family-of-origin work should be discouraged when the client's marriage is not adequately stable.

The consultation process is heavily compromised if there is an active psychotic process in the parental generation. There are similar complications if a parent has a serious physical illness. Situations such as these require special handling on the part of both consultant and client.

Occasionally, an individual continues to feel very deprived emotionally, even in the fourth decade of life. Such an individual may need further active and supportive parenting or reparenting before he or she is able to give up the parents *as parents*. Sometimes a client feels the need to gain or regain the parents as parents in order to be able to give them up. If further parenting is not available from within the family of origin, a substitute therapeutic relationship of a very different order and character may be needed.

Persons who are chronologically adult, but who did not find much opportunity to practice personal autonomy during their developmental years, may find themselves in a kind of values vacuum and decision-making paralysis, once parental domination has been renegotiated. Such a client may be temporarily unable to make significant personal decisions of any kind, constituting an unusual situation that requires some special tolerance by the consultant.

There are particular complications when a client in the fourth decade has a continuing physical or financial dependency on parents. For example, a client may need to use a parental car, to live in a parental home or an apartment owned by parents, or to receive regular financial support for living or college expenses.

Special problems are likely to arise if a parent has been a long-term alcoholic. For this or for other reasons, the parent may feel very guilty about past parenting and may be anxious now to please former children, to the point of being quite obsequious. This obviously makes it difficult to renegotiate and redistribute power in the usual way. One especially difficult version of this occurs when parents adopt very dependent roles and seek to have their former children treat them and care for them as if *they* were children.

Another unusual situation arises when both parents are deceased, although certain debriefing procedures can be used (Williamson, 1978). When only one parent is deceased, the other may be perceived as more vulnerable and, therefore, more in need of support and protection by the second generation. This can complicate the political renegotiation considerably.

From time to time, a client has some dreaded fear or family secret, whether real or imaginary, such as child or spouse abuse, incest, or affairs on the part of one or both parents. Suicidal or homicidal events or attempts in the family, striking vocational-professional failure by one or other parent may also affect consultation.

A unique context develops when parents are deeply suspicious of therapy and therapists or terrified of death and, therefore, of coming into a place where death is inevitably going to be discussed. There are special difficulties with parents who have rigid, fundamentalist religious beliefs and practices, and who, therefore, may be committed to denial as a way of living and being. These parents may interpret all human experience in terms of religious concepts and symbols, thereby denying personal responsibility for any behavior, attitude, or important decision in life made by either generation.

Another unusual circumstance occurs when a son or daughter is homosexual and this fact has not yet been explicitly acknowledged between the client and parents. The client may be unsure that all parties in the relational system will be able to survive the explicit expression of this information, even though it is already covertly available. At the same time, however, the consultant is likely to be convinced that it must be said if consultation is to be a useful process.

The intergenerational consultation is especially difficult when the parents of the client are divorced, particularly if hostility remains a part of that parental relationship. In this case, the client is likely to continue to experience an intense split loyalties dilemma. Another version of this dilemma arises when the client was not raised by the natural parents, but by adoptive parents, and both sets of parents survive.

Finally, the situation is likely to be therapeutically unworkable when the client (or the therapist) is simply too young to be at a developmental point that is appropriate for the renegotiation of these kinds of hierarchical issues. On the other hand, a client may have gone beyond the appropriate point and may no longer have the energy or motivation for this intense emotional investment in change.

Given adequate experience and enough imagination on the part of the consultant, as well as enough preparation time on the part of the two generations involved, all these complex situations can be negotiated, with varying degrees of success. Occasionally, it will be necessary for intentions regarding the final outcome to be more modest, however.

Perhaps the most difficult situation in which to pursue a radical renegotiation of intergenerational politics is that in which there is an active psychotic process in the older generation, or a symbiotic parental connection to son or daughter. In this instance, the psychological organization and equilibrium of the parent may appear to depend on the maintenance of the status quo in intergenerational politics. Usually, this is not true, but it is true that a consultant must be alert and sensitive to the rhythm of the special needs of both generations. The parent's fear of abandonment particularly needs to be addressed and supported.

The second most difficult circumstance occurs when one spouse in a marriage uses family-of-origin consultation to make significant changes in intergenerational politics, while the other stands still or even regresses. In this case, the marital complementarity and interactional balance, at both conscious and unconscious levels, are in jeopardy of being seriously disturbed. In both these instances, the consultant does well to exercise multidirectional partiality (Boszormenyi-Nagy & Ulrich, 1981) with unusual care and patience.

CONCLUSION

Because children see parents as omnipresent and omniscient, they cannot and will not forgive them. Humans do not forgive God. As parents are humanized, mutual forgiveness becomes possible, and forgiveness is a necessary condition of personal freedom in the intergenerational experience.

Obviously, the purpose of the intergenerational consultation includes helping clients to be and increasingly become different from their parents. However, it is also intended to enable clients to be comfortable with being the same as their parents, since this sameness is now chosen and, thus, authentic within the new self. It is only through the experience of personal authority that sameness can be voluntarily chosen.

Experience suggests that a life lived in total commitment to differentiation of self, will end in disappointment and despair. Differentiation of self as a way to self-fulfillment is inherently contradictory. Personal authority in the family system connects intimacy and belongingness to the experience of differentiation, individuation, and relational ethics. Once an adult posture has been taken on the intergenerational stage, however, it is not possible for the client ever again to talk to parents as a child, because the parent no longer exists as a parent for the adult. It may be that, because there is no way back, most people are fearful of taking the step forward.

REFERENCES

Boszormenyi-Nagy, I. Contextual therapy: Therapeutic leverages in mobilizing trust. In R. Green & J. Framo (Eds.), *Family therapy*. New York: International Universities Press, 1981.

Boszormenyi-Nagy, I., & Ulrich, D. Contextual family therapy. In A. Gurman & D. Kniskern (Eds.), *Handbook of family therapy*. New York: Brunner/Mazel, 1981.

Bowen, M. Toward the differentiation of a self in one's own family. In J. Framo (Ed.), *Family interaction: A dialogue between family researchers and family therapists*. New York: Springer, 1972.

Bowen, M. Toward the differentiation of a self in one's family-of-origin. In F. Andres & J. Lorio (Eds.), *Georgetown family symposia: A collection of selected papers*. Washington, DC: Georgetown Family Center, 1974.

Bowen, M. *Family therapy in clinical practice*. New York: Aronson, 1978.

Erikson, E.H. Identity and the life cycle. *Psychological Issues*, 1959, *1*(1), Monograph 1.

Framo, J. Family of origin as a therapeutic resource for adults in marital and family therapy: You can and should go home again. *Family Process*, 1976, *15*, 193-210.

Kerr, M.M. Family systems theory and therapy. In A Gurman & D. Kniskern (Eds.), *Handbook of family therapy*. New York: Brunner/Mazel, 1981.

Paul, N.L., & Grosser, G.H. Operational mourning and its role in conjoint therapy. *Community Mental Health Journal*, 1965, *1*(4), 15-26.

Watzlawick, P., Weakland, J., & Fisch, R. *Change*. New York: Norton, 1974.

Williamson, D.S. New life at the graveyard. *Journal of Marriage and Family Counseling*, 1978, *4*, 93-101.

Williamson, D.S. Personal authority via termination of the intergenerational hierarchical boundary: A "new" stage in the family life-cycle. *Journal of Marital and Family Therapy*, 1981, *7*, 441-452.

Williamson, D.S. Personal authority via termination of the intergenerational hierarchical boundary: II. The consultation process and the therapeutic method. *Journal of Marital and Family Therapy*, 1982, *8*, 23-37. (a)

Williamson, D.S. Personal authority in family experience via termination of the intergenerational hierarchical boundary: III. Personal authority defined, and the power of play in the change process. *Journal of Marital and Family Therapy*, 1982, *8*, 309-323. (b)

Williamson, D.S. Systems-oriented, small group, family-of-origin family therapy: A comparison with traditional group psychotherapy. *Journal of Group Psychotherapy, Sociology and Psychodrama*, Winter 1983, 165-177.

6. Divorce along the Family Life Cycle

David Kantor, PhD
Director
Kantor Family Institute

Clinical Director
The Family Center
Cambridge, Massachusetts

Michael I. Vickers, PhD
Kantor Family Institute

Clinical Director
Divorce Resource and Mediation Center
Cambridge, Massachusetts

IN VIEW OF THE RISING DIVORCE RATE AND THE GROWING RECOGNITION of the influence that divorce has on modern family life, it is surprising how little family therapists have contributed to the understanding and therapy of divorce. Among existing efforts are Keith and Whitaker (1977), Napier (1977), and Bloch (1980), all of whom have described their therapeutic efforts with divorcing families. In addition, Kaslow (1981) has reviewed the literature and concepts of divorce therapy, while Beal (1980) has begun the process of identifying the experiences of divorcing families at differing life stages.

A SYSTEMIC VIEW OF DIVORCE

While systems can evolve without significant crisis, basic system change always begins with crisis. An important distinction is made here between *evolution,* which occurs without crisis, and *transformation,* which is rooted in crisis. The distinction is made in order to try to account for the actual process whereby a family model or paradigm emerges over time from the purposive interactions of its members, all of whom are potential model builders.

John and Mary are married, or, in any case, they are in a continuing, historically stable relationship. Each wants to be and is responsible for creating the system known as the John and Mary Jones Family System. John and Mary make a friend of Rodney, who is frequently in trouble emotionally. John and Mary both value not only friendships, but also the claims friends can make on one's time and resources. As Rodney and other friends bid for their time and resources, John and Mary respond predictably. They gradually become affectionately known as the John and Mary Jones Island of Solace. Their images of demand are compatible; their system structures for dealing with friendships evolve without crisis.

In the case of system evolution, then, family structures emerge when new situations put the family members and the images called forth in them by the situation to the test, and the images coincide more or less. In response to new situations, structures that were not previously present, but are potentially active, are called into existence without struggle or crisis. Systemic differentiation, rather than transformation, is the result. In the evolutionary differentiation, the system remains stable, by and large, isolating the issue (for John and Mary, ''How do we deal with demanding friends?''), identifying it as a nondisruptive demand (''We both agree that friends have incursive rights.''), and establishing a strategic response or systemic pattern that does not require either individual or system reorganization. A structure evolves that does not require struggle, resolution, or the development of a new set of laws.

System change is crisis-based, that is, based on a transformation of individual image elements into new system structures, in most families. A crisis is a temporary breakdown of the internal structure or structural laws governing the system. Such crises occur when individuals in intimate systems bring to bear competing rather than compatible images in response to new situations. Kantor detailed the process by which such crises contribute to the formation of new structures throughout the family life cycle (see Article 2).

Divorce is a special kind of crisis. In the normal developmental process, evolutionary or transformational, the structural changes that take place are progressive. Not only does the system have the ability to regain stability and to recover its character and unity after periods of disequilibrium, but also it has, or develops, the capacity to recognize, tolerate, and respond to the elements that challenge its existing structure, progressively building on and from the crisis elements. Systems crises that eventuate in divorce fail in this regaining of stability and, in most instances, run an unmistakably regressive course, which can be tracked through several stages.

In the first stage, the periods of cyclical disequilibrium begin to dominate, increasing in frequency and duration. In the second, a new element is introduced (e.g., a lover is discovered, a precious heirloom is destroyed, a child is brutalized or molested, a friend's demand for help is dismissed).

Thus far, the crisis process is not very different from that of normal development, but the new element plays a key role in terms of the outcome of the crisis. The critical factor is not the event itself (the discovered lover, the destroyed heirloom) but the meaning of the event. Whereas both in normal development and in the divorce process the disturbance of rules is fueled by a disturbance of basic meaning, in the latter there is a supreme violation of a critical identity image. The rule disturbance persists, and the new element thereby gains a firmly entrenched place in the system, keeping it in a form of runaway.

This signals the third stage. Once the new element becomes entrenched, it keeps the system under constant stress. Both parties—the image violator and the imagistically aggrieved—feeding on the potential of the new element for disturbing the rules, cooperate to keep the system in a state of dynamic imbalance.

In the rather crucial fourth stage, in response to the crushing pressure of accelerating cycles of instability, the system reaches a level of critical disturbance of equilibrium. Naturally, systems vary in their internal criteria for a critical disturbance level. This level is surprisingly high, however, even in times like the present when a lowered level is socially sanctioned. It is as if one or the other partner sends out a signal calling the system's cycle-ending mechanisms into play and the call is answered by the other.

The fifth stage of the divorce process begins when one or both partner(s) either endorse(s) the rule-disturbing element or simply refuse(s) to help isolate it so as to provide relief from the pain and pressure of operating at the level of critical disturbance of equilibrium. Divorcing individuals report a moment of decision that seems to formalize this stage of the divorce process. It is more difficult to "rescue the marriage" of a couple who enter therapy in the fifth stage of the divorce-bound process, even if they come with that goal in mind. At this point, therapy's capacity for restructuring is significantly diminished.

Symptom Formation

One false alternative to restructuring in the face of the divorce-bound system crisis is the development of symptomatic behavior in one or more of the system's members. Symptoms elegantly disguise the nature of the crisis by distracting the system from its disequilibrium. The reframing operations of family therapists should be designed to put the system back into contact with its true developmental crisis and to expose the crisis within a supportive and creative environment.

Divorce is a radical form of system transformation and, in a sense, can be considered an alternative to denial of the underlying crisis. Denial of a crisis could lead to symptomatic behavior in one of the partners or the triangulation of a child. Some divorces occur when a family member no longer accepts the denial of system crisis and attempts to escape "identified patient" status. In other instances, divorce is initiated by one spouse's frustration at not being able to bring the other out of an identified patient status (and its associated life style) obtained in that partner's own family of origin.

Divorce as a Progressive Process

It has been intimated that divorce is a regressive process, by and large. Some divorcing couples feel that they are ending their marriage in order to "grow up," however. Divorce can be seen as a progressive process that allows individual growth or differentiation when, for example, a man informs his wife after 14 years of marriage that he has been bisexual and wishes to choose the homosexual route. It may also be a progressive process for a young couple whose 2-year marriage was formed more out of an ideological conversion in a commune in which they had lived than out of an intimate attachment. In these cases, the divorce decision may be seen as a more or less healthy sign of self-differentiation, a challenge to the authenticity of the couple system identity that had evolved.

Divorce as a Regressive Process

If it is said that all open/living systems naturally gravitate toward greater complexity and differentiation, then divorce may be understood to be regressive at the system level. It transforms the family in a way that prevents the further differentiation of most system elements, although, arguably, it permits growth to continue in some.

One aspect of this regressive process can be viewed as more or less objective: an impairment of the ability to resist destructive disequilibrium (change?). As formerly effective rules for regulating disturbances no longer work and conflicts become more arbitrary, instability itself is institutionalized. Another aspect is more or less subjective: with repeated experience of the inability to stabilize runaway interpersonal process and thereby recover its original form, the system undergoes a change that it, mistakenly, experiences as a change in character.

Loss of Systemic Identity

It appears that every system has an intrinsic character and that each system strives throughout its development to perfect itself as an entity. System distinctiveness does not simply happen, but rather evolves. At any moment in time, however, a system does have an intrinsic character, a principal nature that allows outsiders to recognize this uniqueness and wholeness, as well as to distinguish it as an entity different from others of its type. For those in the system, this essence, or collective identity, has a unifying effect. If it is removed, the system's existential foundation, its direction, and its core purpose is jeopardized.

More than any other single factor, this change in character determines the decision to divorce. After struggles characterized as much by their intensity and ''moral'' integrity as by their duration, most couples do not make the decision to divorce lightly. It is important to remember that these same moral struggles, or identity struggles, are what make development possible. From these identity struggles and the reconciliations of competing identity images, the collective identity (i.e., the system's totality or character) emerges. Indeed, the shaping of a collective identity is one of the central developmental tasks of the intimate system. The hope of preserving what is good about the present collective identity and of molding a better one for the future is what makes the seemingly awesome futility of intimacy struggles tolerable. The decision to divorce is made when the hope of shaping a shared identity is abandoned. This abandonment of hope in the collective identity and the change in character based on the system's inability to recover its original form and nature after a series of identity crises are conceptually and phenomenologically interchangeable.

As discussed earlier, divorce may be seen as progressive when it permits individual levels of self-differentiation. This label is perfectly consistent with the view that divorce is regressive at the system level. This, in short, is the major dilemma of the divorcing couple: whether to sacrifice the life of the family in favor of individual growth.

When the case in point is not obvious, the argument that divorce is a progressive phenomenon may be harder to make, but family therapists, like it or not, are often called upon to do so. That therapists, by their clinical efforts, hold families together who would on their own or with some other therapist agree to separate, is common knowledge. Another known, but commonly ignored, observation is that some therapists move a couple toward divorce who "should" stay together and who would do so with some other therapist. Family therapists must identify their criteria for determining when, in a given developmental crisis, progressive or regressive divorce processes are at work.

A MODEL OF SYSTEM TYPES

The model of system types proposed by Kantor and Lehr (1975) is helpful in viewing the machinations of identity struggles. While studying family homeostasis, Kantor and Lehr identified three distinct forms of systemic organization. These were called, without prejudice, "closed," "open," and "random." Each system type represents a structural form and corresponding set of rules for maintenance and change operations. Thus, while each type goes through change, it does so in its characteristic way.

Closed systems restrict their exchange with their environment, carefully regulating what comes in and what goes out, and basing current behavior and change on relatively known quantities, such as tradition. Open systems' boundaries, on the other hand, may be viewed as semipermeable, permitting greater environmental exchange without abandoning family history. Decisions about what comes in and what stays out of open systems are more likely to be based on participative techniques and interaction among members. Random systems favor spontaneous environmental contacts with few restrictions and a minimum of controlling mechanisms. Ironically, families in random systems are held intact by the support and permission given to members for exploration.

Each system type guides the members' use of space (fixed, movable, and dispersed), time (regular, variable, and irregular), and energy (steady, flexible, and fluctuating). Each of these access dimensions aids the family and its members toward the goals of experiencing affect (fidelity, authenticity, and whimsicality), using power (authority, cooperation, and free choice), and understanding meaning attributed to experience (certainty, relevance, and ambiguity).

The core purpose of closed system families is maintaining stability through tradition. Open systems work toward achieving adaptation through consensus, while random systems support exploration through intuition. It is easy to imagine the fireworks created when one spouse values ambiguity as a goal, while the other attempts to arrive at certainty. There are similar difficulties when a father believes he has failed in his familial duties unless he maintains a position of authority, but the mother undermines his goal because of her own commitment to consensus and lateral communication. In either case, repeated, unintegrated, and unresolved stylistic competition can easily lead to the development of symptoms in one or both partners.

Each system type has been presented in its pure form, which is not always achieved. Problem-free mixed types result from successful resolution of struggles for control over the family model or typal arrangement; flawed versions of each type result from unsuccessful resolutions of such identity struggles. Individual symptoms and other system problems (such as denial of a developmental crisis) usually accompany flawed models.

Families that look "pure" at rest may disclose significant stylistic conflict among members when in crisis. Indeed, our definition of systemic crisis is the temporary breakdown of normal family structural laws. The predictable crises of the family life cycle may elicit structural crises based on struggles over who has control of the family's developing model.

A TASK-ORIENTED FAMILY DEVELOPMENTAL LIFE CYCLE

Whereas many developmental schemas use membership changes as nodal transition points (McGoldrick & Carter, 1982), Kantor based his schema on systemic tasks, focal issues, and dilemmas. Although some of these transition points coincide with changes in membership, the emphasis on the underlying phenomena affecting the family is similar to that in Erikson's (1968) epigenetic life cycle.

The following stages should not be viewed as purely linear or in unvarying chronological order. The tasks were identified by Kantor in clinical observation and validated only through their utility in clinical practice. The stages and their corresponding crises are:

1. attachment—commitment, loyalty, trust, and sexual passion; crisis—the sacrifice of personal prerogative and alteration of previous emotional ties to gain connectedness to a new individual and his or her corresponding social network
2. industry—distribution of labors and assignment of responsibility and authority; crisis—freedom versus constraint and discipline, i.e., how to survive economically and materially both within the household and in the social world beyond
3. affiliation—choosing and accommodating to target social institutions and to rules that govern them, taking into account the family's and individual members' beliefs, values, and meanings; crisis—smaller versus larger identity
4. inclusion—addition of children, pets, furniture, family myths, etc., sharing the resources and making the boundary larger, and deciding how to decide; crisis—availability versus depletion of resources
5. centralization—consolidating, integrating, modifying, and expanding the mechanisms the system has evolved already and continues to evolve for the family's use in facing issues associated with the first four developmental tasks; crisis—suitability versus unsuitability of rules and structures
6. decentralization—opening up boundaries, launching members and letting go, plus attending to existing boundaries, affiliations, industry, and attachments; crisis—loss versus gain
7. differentiation—giving new credence to ''oneness'' within the couple subsystem without unduly threatening the security of attachment; crisis—retraction versus preservation

8. detachment—preparation for not being, letting go graciously without unduly burdening one's family and partner; crisis—the certainty of the need to prepare for death versus anxiety from uncertainty

Failure to resolve dilemmas and accomplish tasks at each developmental stage causes a significant, potentially regressive system crisis. Identity struggles within the family, reflecting system typal differences and brought to the fore by the required confrontation of developmental tasks, are the primary reasons for these crises. If they can be resolved, the family will transform itself accordingly. Otherwise, the family is problem-prone and potentially divorce-bound.

The Therapy of the Divorce-Bound Family System

Although this model of system types and identity struggles can be (and is) used in marital therapy with intact and continuing families (Kantor, 1980), only its use with divorce-bound, or already separated, families will be described here. It is necessary first to clarify identity struggles, thereby "normalizing" them for all family members. This will usually require joining and accommodation by the therapist. Especially in divorce-bound families, joining is difficult because of the decision, or near decision, of each spouse that the other spouse's identity claims are invalid. Thus, the therapist attempting to connect with one spouse creates considerable discomfort in the other. With no other client group does the therapist have to be more sensitive to differences while doing the work of joining.

One solution is for the therapist to take an initial position of neutrality. Although it may appear superficial, such a position really suggests affirmation of all sides to the conflicts and begins, via modeling, the process of clarifying contradictory (but acceptable) identities. A neutral position may be achieved explicitly or implicitly. The explicit form prevents excessive confusion about the therapist's actions, but invites rejection of this move by one or more members. The therapist who is comfortable pushing hard does well with this approach. Implicit assumption of neutrality requires joining with one family member but disguising this joining from another, or alternatively, requesting permission from one to join the other "temporarily." This form works well for therapists who are strong in affective joining and can track the impact of such complex and subtle therapeutic moves.

Experienced therapists might take a "nonneutral" position, which is often a more powerful intervention. Such a position should be preceded by strong joining and a period of demonstrated neutrality, however. It should be set up in an open contract at the outset of therapy and exercised later. The best rationale for therapist bias is that it is the official advocacy of something that goes beyond the couple, such as their children or the good things about their precrisis relationship. Such a bias may be presented as a necessary and useful "antidote to your blindness and madness," a statement that in itself serves as a crude form of reframing.

Before using therapeutic bias, therapists must be clear about the status of typal evolution and struggle in their own family. When therapists have done their "own work," they can more artfully take strong stands, alternately for one, then for the other typal arrangement, around specific issues—what time children go to bed in the other parent's household or when to introduce new partners, for example. A more interesting use of bias occurs when the therapist can personally represent a typal model different from that of either partner. Such therapeutic triangulations are useful in many different kinds of stalled systems, the divorce variety among them.

It is also useful to hold sessions with one family member or subsystem of the family. This further affirms that subsystem and allows the therapist to be seen as a support for that subsystem. One must deal with the implication that repeated individual sessions demonstrate preference, however, as well as with the creation of distance between family members. Generally, such sessions are held infrequently and for specifically stated reasons. Often, children caught in loyalty conflicts can temporarily detriangulate in sessions that exclude both parents, thus gaining some valuable support and guidance from the therapist. Further, sibling subsystems can be restructured to perform some of the functions usually available only from the parents, but not available from them during marital strife.

Therapists' concerns about whether to encourage or discourage divorce, or to take no position, can be approached by reframing the question. How can the family structure be transformed in a way that will work optimally for system members. One useful guideline for directing this transformation is that, as in custody conflicts, this sometimes means finding the "least detrimental alternative." Research on the impact of divorce on children is conclusive enough (Wallerstein & Kelly, 1980) to warrant the assumption that there should be some form of contact between all children and both parents. Another guideline is that parents who prefer the closed system model will appreciate predictable routines, while parents who prefer an open system will want to build in flexibility.

A major goal of divorce therapy, as in most forms of family therapy, is the elimination of any labeling of members as "sick" or the "cause" of family problems. Continuation of such "identified patient" status frequently leads to massive post-divorce conflicts between the spouses and creates obstacles to their formation of new relationships. It is here that the normalizing function of the model of the "causes" of divorce is powerful. Ideally, each family member should leave divorce therapy with a greater awareness that system conflict derives from normal and common life stresses. If they leave with a knowledge of this system type preferences as well, future choices may be made more clearly.

Clinical Work Geared to the Family Developmental Life Cycle

Crisis of Attachment

Bob and Susan M were referred by both of their attorneys for custody consultation. They had been living apart for 5 years, and now Susan was pushing for a divorce. Bob was an attorney himself, although he had not practiced law for many years. Susan was raising their two children without financial support from Bob, but with tremendous animosity toward him. Susan now wanted to remarry; Bob liked the arrangement as it was. The couple had a long-standing agreement for joint physical and legal custody of the children. Susan was asking for sole custody, claiming that Bob not only was a negative influence on the children but also did not deserve custody by virtue of his failure to contribute to their support. Bob argued that his children needed him and that Susan's continued criticism of him was the cause of his unwillingness to cooperate with her.

It became clear that this couple had never had a realistic relationship and that attachments had been formed to highly idealized, unrealistic, and romantic visions of each other. They had met in Paris while on vacations with separate sets of friends and had married in 2 weeks. They apparently enjoyed a honeymoon in France, but serious difficulty began when they planned their return home.

After two couple sessions, individual sessions with each, and individual sessions with each of their two children, the therapist was able to identify this couple's crisis as having originated with a failure of early attachment. For example, the couple fought endlessly over where to reside. Each wanted to live near his or her own family of origin, and each rejected at least one of the other's parents. Thus, it appeared that loyalty was mostly oriented toward their respective biological families. They found little sexual stimulation in contact with one another. Bob favored drinking and moderate drug use as a stimulant and felt that his wife was disappointingly straight-laced in her desire to be romanced soberly with wine and music. Susan saw Bob as a "drug addict" who just wanted to escape reality. Thus, the "diagnosis" of an attachment crisis is strongly supported by the goodness of fit between the theoretically stated dilemma and the couple's data. Additional support was found in the family's inability to resolve the crises at later life cycle stages.

Shortly after their marriage, Susan became pregnant, as she did again about 2 years later. Because of their discomfort with each other, the couple spent little time together. While each participated in child-rearing, they did so unconnected to the other; during the therapy sessions each claimed, with great sincerity, that the other never cared for or about the children. The therapist took the position that they contributed very different things to the children and that, correspondingly, the children were essentially different people with each. Naturally, their concepts of what the children needed from parents varied, as it was based on their own personal typal preferences, as well as on the divergent behavior repertoires each elicited from the children. Had they managed sufficient attachment, they would have had a basis on which to discuss their differing attempts at moving the family through "inclusion."

Industry and affiliation issues were likewise unresolved, but entered. While married, Bob spent much time out of the home with friends, feeling that doing so would provide him with the social life, emotional support, and recreation he needed to maintain his responsibilities. Susan complained that this showed Bob's avoidance of responsibility. Bob claimed that Susan was too compulsive and turned work and chores into slavery.

In terms of their identity struggles, it appeared to the therapist that Susan's preferred system type was close to the closed model, a fairly traditional view of family solidarity and responsibility. Her major energies were happily dedicated to "family." Bob oriented his energy expenditure toward individual spontaneity and separateness, as his way of "stocking up" to make family commitment acceptable. It is important to note that, in doing so, he felt he was supporting family values. In Bob's view, the struggle between personal freedom and familial commitment is best handled by permitting individuals large blocks of free time. In Susan's view, this "dilemma" is handled best by dedicating oneself to the responsibilities and discovering much self-fulfillment in doing so. Bob's system type preferences were possibly open but more likely random.

Because Susan's style dominated the family and even Bob would agree, verbally, to her values, the family was seen primarily as a closed system, but a flawed version of the closed system. Were the system not flawed, there would have been either sufficient agreement for both spouses to achieve their "goals," or a method for absorbing their differences would have evolved. (One example of this would have been for the family to function primarily as a closed system, but for Bob to have been granted "lapses," during weekends perhaps, when he could "forget" responsibilities and it would be okay.)

As it stood, their inability to absorb these differences resulted in Bob's being identified as dysfunctional (irresponsible "druggie"). Both benefited from this labeling in that they were not required to identify their common difficulties in forming attachments. This homeostatic position served the family well until recently, when Susan decided to attempt another relationship.

Bob was deeply committed to his position as the identified patient, which, among other things, gave him permission to be irresponsible in his dealings with Susan and the children. For example, one summer Bob kept the couple's oldest child with him, refusing to return the child at the end of his agreed upon visitation. Bob has thus developed a method of handling the painful separation from his children in a way that does not require him to acknowledge that pain either to himself or to others. The therapist concluded that this systemic "strategy" led to a number of the complaints family members lodged against one another. Bob could not concentrate on developing his career, in part, because of his desperate need to hold on to his family, in turn maintained by his insecurity about the original attachments.

Bob felt immediately enhanced by the therapist's view that he appeared willing to sacrifice career and money in order to maintain ties to his children under such strained conditions. Susan was confused by this, but likewise appreciated the therapist's statement that her sacrifice of free time and dedication to career demonstrated admirable parenting qualities.

Most of the therapy consisted of using different methods to meet the two clients' similar needs. The approach for Bob needed to be more affective than the approach for his wife. He responded well to requests that he share his disappointments with the marriage and his losses around the children. Susan wanted and received straightforward talk about the solutions to specific, concrete problems. Tentatively, the therapist bridged the gap between the couple by asking Susan to see if she could not appreciate Bob's experience of loss, and Bob to recognize Susan's survival level need to see that things were going to work out.

Gradually, the couple's wisdom in separating became reinforced by each one's ability to see and decide against the other's stylistic preferences. Physical distance between them now began to be seen as a relief—a way of coexisting without having to change one another.

Additional sessions focused on ways to help the children adapt to diverse household rules in each residence and the need for the couple to make a commitment to flexibility with regard to potential confusion and error by the cihldren.

When therapy ended, the couple did not have a clear view of how and why they chose one another, but they knew that they were two very different, well-intentioned people not well suited for a mature and intimate attachment.

Crisis of Industry

As a result of identity struggles during the industry phase of the family life cycle, the Fremonts decided to divorce. Eight years after their initial separation, Joan called the therapist, saying that her 16-year-old son, Steven, was becoming extremely negative toward his father, was beginning to fail in school, and was sitting at home alone. She feared that Steven had "poor self-esteem" and was depressed.

Joan had sole custody of the couple's two children, but her former husband, Mark, had been granted liberal visitation rights. Joan reported that Mark was highly irregular in his visits and that the boys gave up counting on him. Occasionally, however, Mark would call them, very angry at them for not initiating contact with him.

During their initial sessions, the couple revealed that Mark changed jobs frequently as a result of "personality problems" with his supervisors. Thus, the family frequently suffered from financial insecurity, if not chaos. Mark felt strongly that the difficulties were the result of business being "cutthroat" and uncaring, but also that it would be entirely improper for Joan to work. For her part, Joan was willing to work if the family required it, but did not feel that she wanted a career. She did feel that it would have been better for her to work than for the family to do without necessities.

Joan and Mark agreed that their initial attraction had been strongly sexual, and positive for both. Indeed, they both felt that their marriage had lasted as long as it did because of this sexual attraction. Joan's first impression of Mark was that he seemed "strong and solid," which meant physically masculine and able to "get to the top." Mark's first impression was of Joan being a "seductress who wanted him to have his way."

While this couple had children, they were never properly included in the marriage. The boys were Joan's. She focused on their dress, eating, and health, while her disappointment with her husband, who struggled endlessly to create a niche for himself in the business world, increased. The couple's failure to address and resolve the tasks and dilemmas of industry was ubiquitous. When his wife's disappointment turned to overt bitterness, Mark took a mistress and soon left the home.

Mark would attend only two therapy sessions, leaving the problem with Steven to his former wife. The therapist succeeded in encouraging Joan to view Steven's behavior as a message to his family and peers. This message was defined as a reminder of the need for family attachments. The discussion of family ties that ensued led Joan to recognize that she needed her son, as she herself was frightened of what life would be like for her as he "moved on." At this point, Steven was brought into the therapy. The therapist proceeded by encouraging Joan to "move on" with her son, into a new form of mothering. In this new form, Joan was to help Steven develop peer and work skills he would need.

After much talk, arguing and confusion, Steven took one of his mother's suggestions and started playing basketball with neighborhood friends. Shortly after, he came home to report that he wanted to take driver's education and that he had heard about a basketball camp he could attend that coming summer.

In the height of enthusiasm, Steven called his father to tell him of his plans. Apparently, Mark was very negative and discouraging toward his son, suggesting that this would probably not work out any better than his previous attempts. Later that summer, Joan called the therapist to report that Steven had done quite well. He had been offered a junior counselor's position for the following season. Furthermore, Joan reported that Mark had visited the camp and had made quite a hit with the boys when he demonstrated his own extraordinary basketball skills. Joan remembered that Mark's "secret" desire was to play professional basketball. Thus, through rediscovering his own attachments to his son, Mark took significant steps toward resolving industry stage crises. This solution took more of an open system form, Mark permitting Steven to find his own way. The therapist speculated that Mark might now permit his own (similar) "passions" to carry some influence in work decisions.

The therapist hypothesized that the Fremonts' marriage reflected a flawed, closed system; because it required traditionally modeled solutions, it was unable to adapt to the demands of life's chores. Had they been able to accept Joan's getting a job or Mark's finding work more closely aligned with his "secret desire," or had they been able to shift roles within the family, with Mark doing more of the parenting and Joan contributing more financially (an option chosen in many open system arrangements), they might have been able to resolve the dilemma at the industry stage, and move on, saving an otherwise workable attachment.

Crisis of Affiliation

The Rossi family experienced an affiliation crisis that they were unable to resolve. Eighteen months after entry into the crisis, George Rossi called the therapist, saying he could no longer tolerate his wife's abandonment of their agreed upon moderate form of Catholicism in favor of the Jehovah's Witnesses. Furthermore he felt his wife, Mara, had become unreasonable and irresponsible. He complained that she had been converted by a team of proselytizers who came to their door repeatedly, over a period of a couple of weeks, and that she began believing she had the "only truth." In addition, Mara insisted that their 4-year-old daughter, Karen, follow all the tenets of the Witnesses, which meant no watching TV, no celebrating birthdays or other holidays, no attending the family's original church, and quitting her day camp in favor of a Witness children's program.

George was deeply distressed. He felt abandoned by Mara, furious at the radicalness of her change and her unwillingness to discuss the family's direction with him, and fearful for his daughter's upbringing and for his relationship with her. To top things off, during the first therapy session, Karen said that her father was "the devil," because all nonmembers were of bad faith and under the devil's control.

George wanted help reestablishing communication with his wife, but Mara refused to attend any therapy sessions, saying there were no problems in the family and that everything was going according to Jehovah's will. George requested the sessions for himself and his daughter, however, hoping that he could be coached to salvage the marriage and his relationship with his daughter.

George and Mara had enjoyed the early years of their marriage. George said they learned disco together and were very popular at a number of night spots they frequented. Both were artists, and they worked together, presenting their work at shows and developing their techniques. The first sign of trouble came with a rift between Mara's mother and her older sister. With the conflict between these two, who had been very close, the long history of arguments between Mara and her mother resumed. Mara responded by criticizing her mother's politics and religious practices and seeking greater contact with her sister. In response, Mara's mother and father effectively cut Mara off, refusing to see their granddaughter.

It appeared that, in large part, Mara made herself available to the Witnesses in response to this conflict with her parents and, further, that she assumed George would join her. The Witnesses may have replaced the feeling of membership, which she had just lost, but they also required an intense religiousness, which contrasted sharply with her parents' (and her husband's) mild approach.

For his part, George refused to validate any aspect of his wife's newfound religion, including her right to choose. His view was that they had a partnership, that decisions must be made jointly, and that major changes were to come about only after much consideration. Mara had thus become cut off from everyone, except her daughter, to whom she clung.

The therapist concluded that Mara's biological family exhibited some characteristics in common with flawed versions of random systems, while George seemed to be operating from within a firmly organized closed system. George experienced satisfaction with religious and extended family ties, but Mara continued within a complex family web of unresolved conflicts. Her family's orientation toward spontaneity and individuality was operating in an extreme form. Choice in regard to extrafamilial affiliations led to the loss of intrafamilial ties. In therapy, George was able to view the conflict as one of system type, thereby letting go of his feeling that Mara's unilateral style was primarily a personal affront to him. Correspondingly, his sense of her as "crazy" changed to the more moderate form of seeing her as "different" and incompatible with him. He dropped his attempt to obtain sole custody of their daughter. A court battle was averted, and custody and property agreements were reached.

Crisis of Inclusion

Peter Aaron entered the therapist's group and then asked for individual consultations for "family problems." Peter refused to invite his former wife and four daughters to therapy, saying "This time it's for me!" Having been separated for 2 years and divorced for 1, Peter and his wife Joan maintained a lukewarm relationship while co-parenting their children. Although they conversed frequently, it was not clear that the two communicated.

Peter's complaints about his family were that they wanted more and more from him. He reported feeling exhausted and uninterested in his work, even though he had been very successful. He felt that he was dragging himself to work to meet his financial responsibilities to his family. This might have been a satisfactory arrangement for him, except for his feeling that his wife and children did not appreciate him. Instead, he felt that they simply expected him to work and provide for them, and that they made no emotional room within the family for him to "let off steam" or complain about being tired or uninterested. He wanted to do something less competitive and more artistic, but no one wanted to help him find a way. Eventually, Peter's resentment led him to change careers. Joan and the children were furious with him, and the girls began missing visitation times. Peter was feeling alone and wanted help in getting through this "next adjustment period."

Over a number of sessions, the therapist learned that, at age 9, Peter had been given up by his parents to his maternal grandmother. While he felt his grandmother was loving and a good parent to him, Peter was plagued with questions and anger at his natural parents. Therapy focused on scenes that were still vivid to him and prepared him to contact his parents, whom he had not spoken to for 30 years, so that he could ask the long-avoided questions.

Peter discovered that his parents were divorced shortly after he moved in with his grandmother. He found that they were unable to resolve or tolerate a great deal of arguing, some of which ended up in physical fighting. His father had been an alcoholic unable to work, and his mother spent her time in a local factory working for a pittance, most of which she gave to her own mother to support Peter. Peter felt inspired by his mother, but furious at his father. Now he felt he was not doing enough for his own family. A joint session was arranged for Peter and Joan.

The couple agreed that their conflicts dated to the birth of their first child. At that time, they began to reveal to each other their views of child-rearing and division of other tasks. Joan wanted to quit work and be a full-time mother. She wanted Peter to continue in his career and to be successful. She said that her mother and father had done things this way and that it had worked well for them. After a number of sessions dedicated to the theme introduced by Peter, "I'm not your father," the therapist succeeded in reframing the problem.

The therapist encouraged the two to see that they had wildly divergent images of how to include a child in their family. Both had strong and unyielding views, supported by intense emotional experiences. Peter had given up on family ties, adopting an angry, "OK, I'll take care of myself!" position, which was compatible with adult relationships because they did not involve dependency demands by others. He might have tolerated fathering and work responsibilities, but only if it had been possible for him to be sufficiently self-oriented. Joan's view of parenting was an extreme of self-sacrifice and not well suited to Peter's. Joan's system preferences were probably closed, judging from her strong family/sacrifice perspective. Peter's was likely open, as he wanted each family member's needs to be recognized.

Crisis of Decentralization

Enid and John French separated when their oldest child, John, Jr., turned 16. They viewed their son's transition into adulthood quite differently. John, Jr. was a pleasant boy who seemed to get along with everyone, at home and at school. He was not outstanding, but played some sports and got by academically. On his 16th birthday, John, Jr. applied for a learner's permit and signed up for driver's education. An old-standing, unresolved conflict re-erupted. In the past, when this conflict arose it had not been significant or of crisis proportions. This time it was.

John, Sr. felt that his son was not yet ready to handle the responsibilities of driving. He viewed John, Jr.'s accomplishments to date as meager and tenuous. He thought it was okay to take driver's education, but that he should not plan to drive the family car for quite a while. John, Sr. laid out a rigorous plan for his son to practice driving in parking lots and to study the driver's manual. John, Jr. reacted to all this mildly, if not meekly, as he had in the past when his father set his curfew earlier than that of his friends, and when he had to study and re-study his assignments at his father's insistence. What was different this time was Enid's reaction.

Enid had always been unhappy with her husband's approach to their son. She believed children should be accepted as they are and that they would learn and grow, naturally. She was angered by what she felt was John Sr.'s distrusting and discouraging attitude. Overriding these feelings, however, was Enid's firm opinion that she should not interfere in the relationship between her husband and her son. Her own father and brother had been very close and did well together. So, until now, she kept quiet.

John, Sr.'s father had died when John was just a few years old. He carried a magical image of him—a war hero well-known and loved in his small New England home town. Even after all these years, John, Sr. missed his father and could not remember a single day he had not thought about him. John, Sr. wanted to provide for his son what he himself had missed.

Enid had been in individual therapy and was encouraged to organize a family meeting to discuss driving privileges and other business. She felt this approach to be natural for her, but knew her husband would not be comfortable with it. She insisted though, "for John, Jr.'s sake." At that meeting, after much heated conversation, a vote was taken. Four votes were cast for giving John, Jr. the right to drive the family car if he passed driver's education and met other legal requirements. One vote was cast against. Upon losing that vote, John, Sr. left the meeting still refusing permission for his son to drive. Previous therapy had not identified John, Sr.'s preference for closed system strategies.

As other issues arose, the gap between Enid and John, Sr. widened. Arguments became more heated, and John, Jr. began taking sides with his mother. An attempt at couple therapy failed after a few meetings, and John, Sr. left the home shortly after.

The family was referred to the therapist for post-divorce counseling. Enid had been offered a job on the West Coast and wanted to move there with the three children. John, Sr. had a job and family connections in the East and wanted to stay. The couple had joint custody of all children and were in the midst of a court battle.

It was felt that the key lay in understanding John, Sr.'s "holding on" to his son as the loving act of a father who wanted his son to have more, not less. The family was convinced that John, Sr. was selfish and negative, discouraging John, Jr.'s attempts to grow up. In spite of the angry gulfs between family members, John, Sr.'s affection for his son, his desire not to lose him, and his continuing sadness over the loss of his own father proved to be powerful factors.

John, Sr. was portrayed by the therapist as preferring a closed system style, but having been thrown askew by his father's death. The impact of that loss was presented as having driven him to place such a high value on family connectedness that the necessary disconnections of adolescence were being overlooked. Enid was portrayed as being oriented primarily to an open system. She wanted her children to make decisions for themselves and was therefore comfortable with her earlier (precrisis) perception that the relationship between her husband and her son was functioning with a large degree of independence from the rest of the family. She began to see that dyad was no longer independent when it conflicted too strongly with her imagery around decentralization. The family meeting outvoted John, Sr. (once again) on the issue of the move, but this time he was given something before it ended. It was agreed that Enid and the children would move, but that everyone would share the responsibility of keeping John, Sr. connected with his children. Telephone calls and travel would be encouraged. It was decided that plane fare would be considered a family necessity, not a luxury, and that John, Sr. would be welcome to stay at the family home on his trips west. While John, Sr. was not truly pleased with the outcome, he was relieved to find his presence was desired by his son and agreed that the arrangement was more satisfying than a court's decree ordering the relationship to continue.

Crisis of Differentiation

Betty and Paul Roan called the therapist to ask for help in separating. They were in their late 50s, with three grown children, and had been arguing for years. Betty explained in the first interview that she had stayed with Paul until the children were grown, and then some, but now wanted to go her own way. Paul wanted an early retirement in the Sun Belt, while Betty was just building momentum in her new career as a realtor in New England. Betty felt that she had done the "wifely" and "motherly" thing for almost 30 years, and now she wanted to catch up on some things for herself. She said Paul was her "only love" but that she just could not adjust his needs to suit hers. Paul could not understand why, after all this time, Betty would leave him. He said he could not imagine life without her, but felt terribly torn. He also could not imagine many more years of work and winters!

After numerous sessions it was clear that neither was about to change the plans for the future, nor would either accept compromises. In fact, it seemed that the therapy sessions intensified the couple's arguing. The therapist fought for the relationship until he realized he was in the way of progress. The inevitable was faced, with much outpouring of emotion. Betty talked about her childhood—dashed dreams and forced training for wifehood. Paul's was more of accomplishments and escalating ambition, with a reward imagined at the end of the rainbow. Florida was to be Paul's reward, but he did not expect to enjoy it alone. Perhaps the time will come, they agreed, for Betty to join him.

AN AFTERWORD

Divorce represents a couple's failure to resolve specific developmental tasks that occur throughout the family life cycle. Any one of these normal developmental dilemmas can be the basis for system crisis, and failure of the therapist to identify the developmental issue at root in the couple's conflict can result in inefficient therapy or even worse, serious mismanagement.

Those who conduct therapy from a developmental perspective assume some responsibility for getting derailed families back on their developmental tracks. It is theoretically, clinically, and ethically insufficient to assume, however, that relieving a symptom or resolving a problem automatically places a family back on course. Nondivorcing families with their presumably more stable internal resources are perhaps able to deal with this sort of clinical oversight. Should a family be so disabled as to become divorce-bound, their presumably dysfunctioning internal resources will be less able to survive a clinical policy that ignores developmental issues.

REFERENCES

Beal, E.W. Separation, divorce, and single-parent families. In E. Carter & M. McGoldrick (Eds.), *The family life cycle· A framework for family therapy*. New York: Gardner Press, 1980.

Bloch, D.A. Divorcing: Clinical notes. In M. Andolfi & I. Zwerling (Eds.), *Dimensions of family therapy*. New York: Guilford Press, 1980.

Erikson, E.H. *Identity, youth and crisis*, New York: Norton, 1968.

Kantor, D., & Lehr, W. *Inside the family*. San Francisco: Jossey-Bass, 1975.

Kantor, D. Critical identity image: A concept linking individual, couple, and family development. In J.K. Pearce & L.J. Friedman (Eds.), *Family therapy: Combining psychodynamic and family systems approaches*. New York: Grune & Stratton, 1980.

Kaslow, F.W. Divorce and divorce therapy. In A.S. Gurman & D. Kniskern (Eds.), *Handbook of family therapy*. New York: Brunner/Mazel, 1981.

Keith, D., & Whitaker, C. The divorce labyrinth. In P. Papp (Ed.), *Family therapy: Full length case studies*. New York: Gardner Press, 1977.

McGoldrick, M., & Carter, E.A. The family life cycle. In F. Walsh (Ed.), *Normal family processes*. New York: Guilford Press, 1982.

Napier, A.V. Follow-up to the divorce labyrinth. In P. Papp (Ed.), *Family Therapy: Full length case studies*. New York: Gardner Press, 1977.

Wallerstein, J., & Kelly, J.B. *Surviving the breakup*. New York: Basic Books, 1980.

7. Families of Remarriage: The Weaving of Many Life Cycle Threads

Mary F. Whiteside, PhD
Ann Arbor Center for the Family
Ann Arbor, Michigan

Many members of remarried families visit mental health clinics. They come in with the full range of symptoms and family life problems. They are presented as personal problems, but they must be considered in the context of the family structure. The strains of living as a part of a remarried family take common patterns. Although the participants do not usually understand the relationship of their complaints to their unique family structure, the therapist must become acquainted with the family network in which the difficulties are expressed in order to plan effective treatment. This, of course, is no easy task. In a remarried family, membership is not defined in any straightforward manner. The unit is not determined by primary emotional bonds or loyalties, legal ties, economic support, or physical residence.

For clinical purposes, the definition of a remarried family unit proposed by Sager and associates is a useful one:

> We define the Rem [remarried] family as one that is created by the marriage (or living together in one domicile) of two partners, one or both of whom have been married previously and was divorced or widowed with or without children who visit or reside with them. The couple and the children (custodial or visiting) comprise the Rem family system. The ''metafamily'' system is composed of the Rem family plus former spouses, grandparents, step-grandparents, aunts, uncles, and others who may have significant input into the Rem system. (Sager, Walker, Brown, Crohn, & Rodstein, 1981, p. 3)

For a person living in this special extended family, a sense of belonging can be elusive. An examination of the remarried family unit and the metafamily system can be very helpful in clarifying a family member's experience.

In both the professional and the popular literature of the past 5 years, the strengths and vulnerabilities of remarried families have been differentiated from those of families of first marriages. Nevertheless, the development of cultural guidelines, traditions, and rituals to shape these families and to determine their relationships with the broader community is only beginning. Visher and Visher (1979) have been particularly instrumental in formulating a model of the remarried family. They summarized the major defining characteristics of remarried families with children as follows:

1. An adult couple is in the household, but a biological parent is elsewhere.
2. The relationship between one adult (parent) and child predates the marriage, and one adult (stepparent) is not legally related to a child (stepchild).
3. Children are members of more than one household.
4. Virtually all members have recently sustained a primary relationship loss.

The implications of these characteristics, as summarized by McGoldrick (1980), are (a) complex, conflicting, and ambiguous new roles and relationships; (b) complex and ambiguous boundaries of the system; and (c) intense conflicted feelings, or denial of them.

Construction of a satisfying remarried family and metafamily system is a creative endeavor. Remarried family members must deal with historical definitions of family, parenting, and patterns of loss and separation from families of origin, from the first marriage, and from two single-parent households. The definition of the remarried family unit begins during courtship and is revised and developed through the marriage ceremony and beyond. Each new family event, e.g., births, custody changes, the former spouse's remarriage, graduation, children's marriage, and deaths, presents unanticipated complexities and challenges the family members to create new ways of living together.

Clinical intervention begins with an understanding of the remarried family model. There are several excellent beginning texts that delineate common stepfamily issues and present clinical suggestions (e.g., Crohn, Sager, Rodstein, Brown, Walker, & Beir, 1981; Einstein, 1982; Sager et al., 1981; Visher & Visher, 1979). As therapists continue to work with this view of remarried families and as families continue to describe their adaptive solutions, the range of clinical ideas will become much richer. Several authors have begun to place remarried families into a life cycle perspective; for example, organizations of developmental stages for remarriage have been presented by McGoldrick (1980); Messinger and Walker (1981); Ransom, Schlesinger, and Derdyn (1979); and Whiteside (1982b). In addition, Beal (1980), Wallerstein and Kelly (1980), and Weiss (1975) have begun to map the experiences of family members moving from marital separation through two single-parent households.

Like all other issues in the remarried family, a life cycle perspective immediately becomes complex and ambiguous. Evidence is accumulating, however, that most people go through fairly regularly occurring sequences as they move from the family of first marriage to the family of established remarriage. Each stage in the process is part of a cycle. A critical shift occurs, disrupting the ongoing stable relationship pattern. An unsettled period of transition follows, out of which emerges a new equilibrium, only to be followed by a new cycle of change. Each stage has its own challenges, tasks to be accomplished, and timing. The solutions adopted in early stages affect the patterns of coping and points of vulnerability in succeeding stages. To complicate matters, however, the two families coming together for remarriage may be at different points in the marriage-divorce-single-parent household sequence. They may differ in the amount of unresolved emotional baggage that is brought along from the first marriage (or from the family of origin) as well as in the degree of stability or entrenchment that has developed in the parent-child unit.

Family members can be placed within the traditional family life cycle framework (Duvall, 1971; Hill & Rodgers, 1964) according to the age of the children, the point of the first marriage, the age of the adult, and the point in the adult's employment career. The remarried family goes through developmental sequences related to the age and stage of the individual family members as well as those related to the divorce and remarriage. The two developmental sequences interact with one another, producing complicated and contradictory results. For example, much has been written about the important tasks introduced into a marriage by the birth of the first child. What happens when the first child of the marriage is the third child for the wife, but the first for the husband, who thus has none of the familiarity and experience, but all the awe, excitement, and disruption of becoming a new parent?

Further interactions come from the fact that the experience of divorce and remarriage is different for children of different ages. In addition, the child's experience may be very different from the adult's experience, even though they are both going through the same time frame. The remarriage may be bringing together families at very different life stages and may involve family members with very different reactions. This has implications not only for the families' ability to come together smoothly, but also for the eventual structure possible for the remarried family. The role of stepparent to an adolescent is different from that of stepparent to a very young child. The stepparent can play a more intimate role in the development of a young child, a role that is more parentlike. Because of this, however, the stepparent to a young child may be more vulnerable to the myth that it is possible to create a "nuclear family," denying the importance of both natural parents in the child's life and the child's own split longings.

In sum, there can be no neatly presented developmental sequence for the remarried family that will take the many family variations into account. The first clinical task, therefore, is an assessment one. The therapist maps with a family the relationships within their metafamily and becomes acquainted with the various intersecting life cycle positions represented.

Figure 1 illustrates a time line that can be useful in locating a family within common life cycle events and in developing an initial idea of the issues with which the family may be struggling. Important structural organizations along the time line (indicated by circles) are

1. the two-parent first family—a system that developed a merged "culture" from the two families of origin and has its own patterns of nurturance, division of labor, family boundaries, and system of relationships.

2. the dual single-parent household—two separate subsystems that are part of a new extended family. The effort at merging into a common culture has been abandoned. Each parent is taking charge of his or her own household, although important pieces of the history of the first family are maintained. The children have the difficult task of integrating for themselves the values and relationship patterns from two separate households. The parenting function must now be organized across household boundaries or, with the older children, across generation boundaries; the adult needs to obtain support and adult stimulation outside the immediate household, yet not from the former spouse.

3. the remarried family—a subsystem of a now even larger metafamily system. The sharing of household and family responsibilities between adult partners is returned to household boundaries, and generation boundaries are redefined. Financial and parental functions are still shared across households, which may be complicated by the presence of yet another outside household when both spouses have children from previous marriages. Again, there is the task of merging two family cultures.

At each of these points of family organization there is a wide variety of family styles and structures. Each pattern has different implications for the transition into the remarried family. The transition periods between the three stable configurations are long and painful. During periods of reorganization, families cannot rely on time-worn strategies for working together. There is no sense of stability, and there are no rules for comfortable closeness or for reasonable distance. There are no predictable times for refueling or familiar

Figure 1 Common Life Cycle Events for the Remarried Family

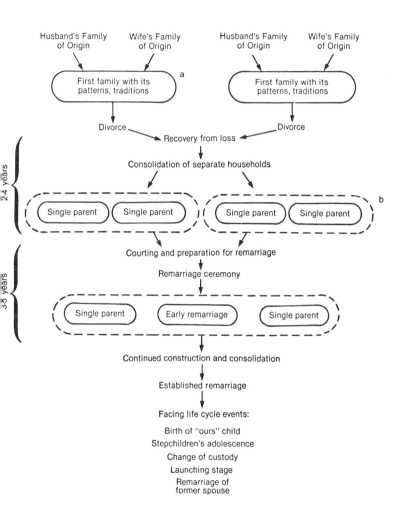

a Family unit indicated by ——

b Metafamily unit indicated by ------

patterns for arguments. Strong emotional responses are triggered in all family members. Without a sense of family unity or identity, members feel separate and isolated.

COURTING AND PREPARATION FOR REMARRIAGE

The time of preparation for remarriage is an important one. If moves are taken gradually, perhaps over a year (Einstein, 1982), the first few months after the two families move in together may be less difficult. The tasks of this period are the continued resolution of the first marriage, the gradual modification of the single-parent household structure, and the anticipation of the remarried family structure.

Resolution of the First Marriage

Kressel and Deutsch (1977) suggested that a divorce is "constructive" when each partner has a balanced view of the other and of the marriage, an increased self-understanding, a heightened sense of personal competence, the ability to form satisfying new intimate relationships, and the ability to maintain a good co-parenting relationship for the children. Wallerstein and Kelly (1980) suggested a concept of joint parental responsibility described as "two committed parents, in two separate homes, caring for their youngsters in a postdivorce atmosphere of civilized and respectful exchange" (p. 310). Beal (1980) added the three-generational perspective, suggesting that the more supportive and nonpolarized the involvement of the extended family, the better the resolution in the marital dyad.

Constructive divorce and positive co-parenting provide the strength and the flexibility necessary to cope with the even more complex and tangled emotional tasks of remarriage. If there is continued bitterness between former spouses their strong emotional attachment continues and makes constructive resolution of differences in the new marriage much less likely. Continued fights over custody, visitation, and child support keep the children in turmoil, fuel intense loyalty conflicts, and make it unlikely that the children will be able to build a new relationship with a stepparent.

The process of becoming intimately involved with and committed to a new person is made possible by the resolution of the attachment from the first marriage. The new relationship also facilitates giving up the marriage. During courtship, there may be a resurgence of feelings about the old marriage on the part of both former spouses. Thoughts of a second marriage bring up a review of the first marriage, even though the divorce has been worked through carefully and constructively. One young woman found herself staying late into the night, talking and drinking with her former husband and his wife-to-be, saying goodbye again on the eve of his remarriage. Despite her approval of the new marriage, she found herself angry and depressed on the wedding day. All the neighborhood friends were going to the wedding, and she felt renewed feelings of aloneness and isolation. Another woman found herself inexplicably tense and angry before meeting her future new mother-in-law. Only later, surprised and elated over the woman's friendliness, did she remind herself of the tensions and disappointment she had experienced with her first mother-in-law.

Modification of the Single-Parent Household Structure

The courting process allows the participants to experiment with the roles of new partners with seriousness, yet with the ability to retreat and then to reach out again. Weiss (1979) described the gradual movement into the household of a single mother's boyfriend as a shift from "helping out" to "sharing responsibility." The advantages of the single-parent unit are a strong sense of independence and freedom, time for peaceful solitude, and close, mutually supportive ties with the children. Despite the overload and strain of this organization, the advantages have been hard won and are not easily relinquished. The attraction of the happiness, companionship, and potential security of the new marriage is strong, but the fears and resistance can be equally intense. A sharing of responsibility entails modification of everyday routines, financial decisions, and parental relationships—extensive modifications for someone still feeling vulnerable in an intimate relationship.

The period of preparation is a chance to establish friendships with potential stepparents or stepsiblings, without yet having to share the bathroom or to accommodate different household rules. Einstein (1982) suggested that time be spent in family outings and that the children of both families, as well as the adults, be involved in planning for the new living quarters. Pleasurable activities of relatively neutral content allow a sense of cohesion and unity to develop. If experiences can be provided in which everyone has little to lose in terms of past loyalties, but something enjoyable to gain, new patterns of transaction will evolve, providing a stronger base from which the more difficult issues of living together may be approached.

Frequently, the single-parent unit has as an important structural component the role of the parental child, i.e., the child sharing parental responsibilities. Weltner (1982) described the adaptive functions of this role when it is clearly defined, supported, and not overwhelming. He also illustrated the important role of the "family cabinet," the "marshalling of several children to assist mother with executive functions" (p. 206). If these roles have been handled clearly and supportively with permeable generational boundaries, they provide a good model for independence and working together to establish family rules and responsibilities in the remarried family. A remarried family carrying on these patterns, however, must be organized to accommodate independent children who share substantially in the executive decisions of the household. The skills and maturity of these children must be acknowledged in the new family, or they will feel displaced, angry, and resentful. For a new stepparent, particularly one without experience with adolescents, the implications of reduced parental authority in such a household may be difficult to accept. If the parent-child unit in the single-parent family is too rigid and is based on the parent's inability to function independently or to find adult support outside the household, there may not be an adaptation to the needs of the remarriage. It will be very difficult for the family to establish a new organization without serious tension and disruption. No matter how adaptively these patterns functioned in the single-parent unit, however, remarriage will be disruptive as space must be made for new family members.

Anticipation of the Remarried Family Structure

As the couple moves closer to remarriage, a host of issues emerges with many more complications than arise for first marriages. Messinger, Walker, and Freeman (1978) described a program of weekly group meetings for couples who were preparing for remarriage. Common concerns expressed in these groups were associated with the transition from separation to marriage; the redefinition of personal identity; the ties between the first and second marriages in terms of finances, custody, and contact with former spouses; the role of the partner in regard to the spouse's children and those of the children in regard to their parent's partner; and expectations for the second marriage based on previous experience. Visher and Visher (1982) and Einstein (1982) suggested that a great deal of planning be done before the marriage in such areas as finances, household rules, child-rearing values, expectations for the marriage, custody decisions, and visitation schedules. McGoldrick (1980) felt that difficulty in making the transition to remarriage could be predicted if any of the following conditions were present: the failure to complete the tasks of separation from the first family, expectations that a remarriage structure will be similar to the structure of a first family, and the denial or lack of awareness of the complicated emotional issues involved in remarried family life for both adults and children.

Families may deny that the marriage will have emotional impact throughout the metafamily; however, it is useful to examine the specific effects that this change will have on the family, predicting reactions and planning explicit ways of acknowledging the change to make feelings more manageable. One woman denied that her former husband would have any feelings about her marriage. When the therapist restated that he might not be showing his feelings directly, however, she agreed with tears of sadness for the lost marriage.

Many parents are surprised by the sudden eruption of discipline problems, withdrawal, or angry tantrums (''You don't care about me!'') on the part of children who have seemed positive and accepting of the upcoming marriage. This comes in part from the mixed feelings children may have about the marriage. They may feel they are losing much more than they are gaining. Every change in the family organization raises the possibility in their minds that they may lose their place in the family or may lose contact with both parents. Also, children are closely attuned to the parental anxieties that arise as the wedding day approaches. Frequently, the children's upset provides a protective function. It confirms an intense, if negative, tie with the parent and draws the parent's focus away from the upsurge of doubts that come as the day approaches. It may be helpful at this time to acknowledge with the child the legitimacy of the child's feelings, to clarify, once again, that the decision to marry is a parental one and not one for which the children are responsible. In addition, the members of each separate family might do something together that directly acknowledges a goodbye to their single family unit, yet reconfirms their continued, if changed, special family ties.

The Wedding Ceremony

Symbolizing the start of the new family, the wedding ceremony can be a joyous occasion that is shared by all and provides strength to cushion future tensions. On the other hand, it may reflect potential problems, consolidating splits that continue over the years. Discussion of the pragmatics of the ceremony—who is doing the planning, what is the couple trying to express through the ceremony, what roles do the children and grandparents play— may help the family clarify their positive vision. Clues to developing emotional splits and alliances, as well as indications of supports or tensions from the extended family may be seen and acknowledged. For one family, a procession of pairs of children from both families symbolized the essential support for the new marriage from the adolescents. For another family, the refusal of two children from the father's first marriage to attend reflected an estrangement that was to cause pain for years to come. It also signaled that loyalties to the first marriage had not yet been put aside.

EARLY REMARRIAGE: CONTINUED CONSTRUCTION AND CONSOLIDATION

The early remarriage period is a time of acute disequilibrium—an experience that runs counter to the expectation of a happy honeymoon period. No matter how carefully and sensitively a family has prepared itself, the time is likely to be unsettling, filled with unexpectedly intense emotions. It is helpful to family members to know that they are going through experiences common to all remarried families, but the knowledge does little to resolve the situation. It appears to take at least 3 to 5 years for a family to stabilize and to "feel like a solid family." Visher and Visher (1979) noted, "It has been said that 40 percent of second marriages end in divorce within four years" (p. xix).

As pointed out by Stern (1978), Visher and Visher (1979), and Whiteside (1982a), each family holds strong beliefs about what is "normal" and "right"—but these beliefs may be different. The task is gradually to develop a new version of family rules and values that feel right in the new family. Stern (1978) terms this the creation of a "sentimental order" within the family. As all the everyday rules must become explicit and consciously discussed, however, family members become anxious and uncomfortable. They may feel that, if all that felt "normal" in the past is subject to discussion and change, all basis for family connection may be dissolved. In spite of this, explicitness has the advantage of creating an openness to trial solutions and input from each family member. Discussing old patterns as just one option in the routine of everyday living may threaten hard-won stability carried over from the single parent unit, but it also neutralizes the intensity of loyalty to former identities so that new alliances may be formed.

Clinical interventions with families in this stage of remarriage must be made with an awareness of these tasks and of the fluidity of the family relationship structure. Efforts at premature closure should be blocked while efforts to restructure the family into a viable unit are supported. Much of the clinical literature dealing with remarried families focuses on this early stage, and many of the critical relationship issues have been well defined. Therapy with families experiencing difficulties at this stage involves dealing with unfinished emotional business from earlier stages, as well as directly confronting the complications of remarried family life and helping to set up decision-making structures and conflict-resolving mechanisms. Particularly important therapeutic interventions at this stage are those that deal with cohesion rituals and distancing rules.

Cohesion Rituals

Reiss (1981) discussed the importance of the "ceremonials of family life," which include "formalized and repetitive patterns that enhance the family's image of itself and express it clearly to its members and nonmembers alike" (p. 226). These patterns, of course, take time to develop in the remarried family. When a family comes in very early in the remarriage and describes a fairly chaotic and separated family life, however, introduction of planned whole family rituals can help stabilize the situation. It may test a family's ingenuity to establish a regular, repetitive event that can involve family members of all age levels meaningfully, and provides an opportunity for them to "feel like a family." It may be an everyday routine, such as a rule that all family members must be home for 6:00 dinner. Alternatively, it may involve more elaborate activities, such as the creation and dramatization of religious stories performed by the six stepsiblings in a newly remarried family.

The couple must be prepared for strong resistance from some family members as they try to carry out this task. Success and good feeling in the remarried family can produce just as much anxiety as the confrontation of differences. Growing feelings of attachment and affection carry with them fears of rejection once again. In addition, movements toward a new alignment signal the loss of the old family, placing family members in the midst of loyalty conflicts.

In the family that includes both custodial and visiting children, regular cohesion rituals should be constructed to support both family groupings. These convey the message that the family is not only a good one with all the children, but also a good one with the smaller grouping. Each subgroup can have important activities that serve as building blocks in the new family construction. Regular routines to be followed when children move between households help to ritualize expression of frustration and sadness, as well as facilitate the transition.

In addition to providing explicit support for new family subgroupings, it is important to continue some rituals established in the single-parent family.

Although a tight boundary that excludes new family members is not an adaptive one, neither is it adaptive to deny the value of the achievements of earlier good times. Particularly for the children, such a denial threatens important aspects of their identities. Family members fear that splitting into the two family subgroups will endanger the whole family cohesion by cementing battlelines. The stepparent may feel threatened if not included. Honoring important historical events and long-standing intimate ties can refuel and add a stability out of which new alignments can be forged, however. If each subgroup feels that they are not required to discard everything, they may be more willing to change some of their former routines. Thus, the father and his children may go on a weekend camping trip, like old times, while his wife and her children have a Saturday night pizza party on the living room floor, as they used to do. All come together on Sunday evening with new energy to live together during the month ahead.

Distancing Rules

Distancing rules are necessary for several reasons. They counteract the myth of instant intimacy, the push to be just like a nuclear family. Distancing rules acknowledge that a couple in a second marriage can be allergic to too much closeness. Such rules underline the fact that stepparents can never feel the same toward their stepchildren as they do toward their natural children and the fact that it takes a long time to build the trust, respect, and friendship on which to base authority. Talking explicitly about ways to maintain distance from one another gives family members a sense of control. They may be more willing to reach out, if they know how to back away and to keep feelings from going too far.

Distancing rules develop within a family along with the cohesion rituals. At first, the two families clash over rules for space, closeness, and distance. What "feels right" to one family in terms of expressing affection, of saying "no," of asking for help, of spending time alone may "feel" quite "wrong" for the other family. The therapist needs to be aware of the existing rules for each person's distance and manner of achieving it. All too often a distancing move may be misinterpreted as "I don't love you" rather than as "If I don't get some space, I'm going to go crazy." Instead of suggesting that a couple increase their level of closeness, which may increase their anxiety level alarmingly, a therapist may be wiser to suggest the need for difference and distance, perhaps commenting, "Are you sure you two can stand that much time together? Perhaps you should stop your discussions after half an hour."

One family may see strength in independent actions. The other family may see strength coming from active support and protection. The validity of both styles of living together should be established, the everyday ways family members are misunderstanding these styles explicitly clarified, and new styles created from a gradual meshing of the old styles. "This is the way my mother always did it," said by a teen-ager may be a statement of loyalty, but it is also a statement of fact. The teen-ager may be expressing 14 years of training in how to get along at home, a training that is being questioned without the provision of a comfortable replacement.

Through the early years of remarriage the family goes through a continuing process in which relationship rules are set, tested with much fireworks, revised, stabilized, then tested anew.

ESTABLISHED REMARRIAGE AND LIFE CYCLE EVENTS

After 3 to 5 years, the remarried family unit has formed a more or less stable structure, perhaps rigid, perhaps resilient. When the family is together, there is no longer a sense of disarray and splintering into unrelated positions; the group has cohesion and organization. In many families, the benefits of increased security, contentment, and loving exchange are evident both for the children and for the adults. Established stepparents may comment on their increasing wisdom and relaxation. Once the pressure to be a daughter is abandoned, a stepdaughter's relationship with her stepmother may begin to bloom on its own. One stepmother described how she was finally able to stop competing with her stepson's natural mother and to encourage him to spend more time with his mother. Surprisingly, she found that, as the boy grew closer to his mother, he also grew closer to her.

Unhappy coalitions may also have solidified. The stepparent may have been closed out of any meaningful relationship with the stepchild, or the child may have assumed a scapegoat position, detouring the couple's difficulties in their own relationship. Despite the stability of the established remarried family, the unique structure and issues remain highly salient and frequently underlie clinical concerns. In addition, normal, predictable life cycle events provide new periods of disequilibrium, challenging the remarried family members.

The "Ours" Child

The birth of a child of the remarried family is generally considered to be a positive force, particularly if the couple have reached a level of stability within their relationship. A symbol of the new family, the baby is the first person who is a blood relation to all members of the family. The anticipation and arrival of the new baby, however, can bring about unexpectedly tense and anxious times for several members of the household.

> In one family, the stepmother had been selected in part for her care and devotion to her husband's child. She had succeeded in maintaining a generally positive relationship with the child until she herself gave birth to a child. Suddenly, she found a great discrepancy between her feelings for her own child and her feelings for her stepchild. Bewildered and guilty, she found herself angry at the stepchild, depressed at what she perceived to be her failure in mothering him, and unable to readjust her perception and actions to fit both mother and stepmother roles. Her husband, who was not a stepparent, could not understand. He blamed her for her unfairness and felt she was rejecting his child.
>
> Compounding the difficulties was the older child's reactions as he worried about the change in the family. He sensed the difference in his stepmother's feelings and feared the worst—there was to be no place left in the family for him. His anxiety accelerated, manifesting itself in distractibility at school and increased misbehavior at home. He protected himself from disappointment by becoming generally unlovable in his actions. For him, the normal sibling reactions were intensified and confused by the added complexities of the steprelationships involved, as well as by the past departures of family members at crisis points.
>
> The child's natural mother, to whom he usually turned for reassurance and clarification, was herself in a bewildering position. She was expected to help her child prepare for a new sibling—one to whom she was not related, had no choice about bringing into the family, and for whom she had no responsibility. Furthermore, the new baby represented to her the unborn children of the first marriage so that her feelings of bitterness, anger, and loss resurfaced.
>
> Finally, since the first marriage had ended during the phase of early parenthood, the anticipation of the new baby stirred up for the husband unresolved difficulties about his ability to be a parent and to co-parent. These anxieties were expressed in increased friction with his former wife and were amplified by her mixed feelings.
>
> The therapist's role in this situation is to examine the issues in all their complexities, remaining sensitive both to the metafamily and to the household members. By placing the situation into perspective as a developmental crisis, while clarifying and supporting as normal the contradictory feelings surrounding the new baby, the therapist frees family members to revise their relationship to accommodate the new family member without sacrificing old family members. In addition, exploring the

patterns that had been functional before the baby arrived and supporting their continuation may reinforce the family's strengths during a relatively unstable time.

In this family, the stepmother was able to resume some of her activities with the boy. The natural mother, with the therapist's support about the unfairness of it all, was able to do the "impossible," that is, to contain the bitterness felt toward her former spouse and act in a way helpful to her child. The father was able to use his new wife's support to continue positive contact with both children, reducing somewhat the disputes with his former wife. With the resulting support from the adults involved, the boy was able to settle down very quickly, becoming quite happy with his new sibling.

Adolescence

When a remarried family includes adolescents, the boundaries around the family are necessarily more permeable because of the longer history of the first families and because of the adolescent's need to establish an independent identity. In addition, there is the importance of acknowledging in decision-making structures the increased power and responsibility of the adolescents as independent household members.

It is not uncommon for the issue of a custody change to emerge as a child enters adolescence in a family of divorce. The child who has been living with the mother in a single-parent household may be having difficulties at home and at school, for example, and the father may have a greater ability to control the adolescent child. There may be a longing to become closer and to know better the noncustodial parent as the adolescent struggles to define his or her identity. This may correspond with the noncustodial parent's new stability through remarriage or with the custodial parent's desire to make a shift in careers that entails increased time away from the children. Alternatively, it may reflect increasing tension in a remarried family in which a pubescent adolescent must deal with opposite sex stepsiblings and a honeymooning pair of parents in very close quarters. Other difficulties in the second marriage may make the noncustodial parent's home seem like a safe haven.

Conceivably, the shift in custody can be an appropriate adjustment to reasonable needs of both adolescent and the families involved. Such flexibility requires anticipation, preparation, acknowledgment of the mixed feelings involved, and cooperation of parents and stepparents. Even with the best preparation, however, there can be residual bitterness on the part of the custodial parent—just as the child is becoming independent and responsible, the child leaves. There may be a sense of parental failure, mutual blame from former spouses at not having fulfilled their parental duties, or resentment on the part of the new household members at having to accommodate a new member just as the family was beginning to settle down. These feelings are particularly likely to emerge if the move takes place as a solution to increased difficulties at home, school, or in the community. The child may feel expelled, unwanted, and unsure that there is an actual home anywhere.

The move requires a shift in both households. The new custodial family must restructure to incorporate the child within its boundaries, and this entry may seriously overload the system. The role of the new noncustodial parent is also altered; a new, more distant, less immediately involved relationship must be built with the child.

Launching Stage

When the child leaves home for college, old difficulties from the first marriage are often rekindled, as child support agreements must be renegotiated. Divorce decrees made years before that required the father to pay, for example, may or may not be honored. This brings the child into direct contact with the father over money and makes the child the focus of old parental arguments. Disagreements may lead to late payment of tuition or disputes over living expenses. Summer vacations become difficult as the mother haggles with the father over living expenses for the child, and the young adult feels unloved, unsupported, and bitter: "I should pay rent to stay at my mother's house?!"

The developmental shift suggests that, instead of having the parents negotiate the support money, the young adult should deal directly with each parent over each one's contribution to college expenses. At this stage, young adults need to know clearly what to expect in terms of family support, required self-support, and the conditions for returning home. For some, there is a long-standing distance from the noncustodial parent, usually the father, and a reluctance to talk with him directly. They then complain to the mother, fueling the still unfinished divorce dispute. Because there is now additional freedom and greater emotional maturity, however, these college-aged children reestablish that important contact with the noncustodial parent. At this age, they may be able to understand more clearly their parents' points of view and the circumstances surrounding the divorce and later marriages.

Frequently, stepparents are extremely helpful to these children. Stepparents may support them by loaning them emergency money to pay the rent while the natural parents are resolving their disputes. They encourage renewed contact with the natural parent—perhaps more freely now because they do not have to struggle with the everyday living situation. They may directly appreciate and support a young adult's accomplishments while the custodial parent is still struggling with ambivalent feelings of loneliness and anxiety over the empty house.

For the whole family, there is a restructuring of relationships as the child becomes more independent and the couple and/or single parent have more time to themselves. Einstein (1982) noted comments from couples who worried that, having spent so many years arguing about the children, they had no positive relationship left.

For the remarried couple, just as for the first married couple, this is a time of freedom that can be used to renew the couple's relationship and to pursue long-postponed activities and career interests. This may be the first time the remarried couple have been by themselves for any extended length of time, however. The couple may be well suited to this transition, since they came to the remarriage with the differentiation and skills gained when they were self-sufficient during the single-parent stage. When the marriage is viewed as a partnership with room for outside activities, and a pleasure in the companionship with one another, their relationship may flourish. Alternatively, the strains and consolidated distances from the turbulent early remarried years may have seriously weakened the couple's relationship; cracks and unfulfilled expectations may come into clear view when they have time to look at each other.

LATER REMARRIAGE

As discussed by McGoldrick (1980), the couple who remarry later in life, after their children are married with children of their own, face the difficulties caused by very long histories in first families, numerous complicated family ties, and questions of financial arrangements, wills, and inheritances. Reactions from adult children remain surprisingly strong, although they support their parent's decisions for a happier life. Again, there is evidence of the typical 3- to 5-year time span before a group of unrelated strangers who have mixed feelings can develop the feelings of a connected extended family. One woman reported a family reunion around her father's birthday, 4 years after his remarriage, that for the first time included both her siblings with their families and her stepsiblings with their families. She linked this not only to the passage of time, but also to her father's recently increased involvement with his wife's children.

CONCLUSION

Each stage in the first family through established remarriage provokes a family reorganization in a very complex and challenging network of relationships. It poses unusually contradictory and unexpected feelings. These contradictions do not disappear, but the increasing stability and confidence in flexible arrangements may make each transition less crisis-prone. Each stage provides the opportunity for a flareup of the feelings from the first marriage, but also an opportunity to understand in a different manner, and to realign contacts in a more satisfying way. As emphasized by Wallerstein and Kelly (1980), there are repeated and enduring efforts at mastery on the part of all family members which come into play at each developmental stage.

Developmental transitions come from changes in the remarried family, from changes in the metafamily surrounding the remarried unit, and from changes for each of the individual members. Therapeutic interventions can support the process most usefully if they are made within the context of the metafamily network and with an awareness of the tasks appropriate to each stage of the remarried family. Early stages of the remarriage require interventions which facilitate the development of a "sentimental order" within the new family, which acknowledge the strengths carried over from previous family organizations, and which normalize the feelings of tension, confusion, and frustration. Both cohesion rituals and distancing rules need attention. Events which occur later in the remarriage can also be dealt with most fruitfully within a developmental perspective as the therapist explores with the family the special contradictions and complications which arise within the stepfamily constellation in the course of normal changes. Each transition requires the family to reach back into its history, to review past solutions, and to clarify and construct relationships in new patterns to meet the current challenge.

REFERENCES

Beal, E.W. Separation, divorce, and single-parent families. In E.A. Carter & M. McGoldrick (Eds.), *The family life cycle: A framework for family therapy.* New York: Gardner Press, 1980.

Crohn, H., Sager, C.J., Rodstein, E., Brown, H.S., Walker, L., & Beir, J. Understanding and treating the child in the remarried family. In I.R. Stuart & L.E. Abt (Eds.), *Children of separation and divorce: Management and treatment.* New York: Van Nostrand Reinhold Co., 1981.

Duvall, E.M. *Family development.* New York: Lippincott, 1971.

Einstein, E. *The stepfamily: Living, loving, and learning.* New York: Macmillan, 1982.

Hill, R., & Rodgers, R.H. The developmental approach. In H.T. Christensen (Ed.), *Handbook of marriage and the family*. Chicago: Rand McNally, 1964.

Kressel, K., & Deutsch, M. Divorce therapy: An in-depth survey of therapists' views. *Family Process*, 1977, *16*, 413-444.

McGoldrick, M. Forming a remarried family. In E.A. Carter & M. McGoldrick (Eds.), *The family life cycle: A framework for family therapy*. New York: Gardner Press, 1980.

Messinger, L., & Walker, K.N. From marriage breakdown to remarriage: Parental tasks and therapeutic guidelines. *American Journal of Orthopsychiatry*, 1981, *51*, 429-438.

Messinger, L., Walker, K.N., & Freeman, S.J.J. Preparation for remarriage following divorce: The use of group techniques. *American Journal of Orthopsychiatry*, 1978, *48*, 263-272.

Ransom, J.W., Schlesinger, S., & Derdyn, A.P. A stepfamily in formation. *American Journal of Orthopsychiatry*, 1979, *49*, 36-43.

Reiss, D. *The family's construction of reality*. Cambridge, MA: Harvard University Press, 1981.

Sager, C., Walker, E., Brown, H.S., Crohn, H.M., & Rodstein, E. Improving functioning of the remarried family system. *Journal of Marital and Family Therapy*, 1981, *7*, 3-13.

Stern, P.N. Stepfather families: Integration around child discipline. *Issues in Mental Health Nursing*, 1978, *1*, 50-56.

Visher, E.B., & Visher, J.S. *Stepfamilies: A guide to working with stepparents and stepchildren*. New York: Brunner/Mazel, 1979.

Visher, E.B., & Visher, J.S. *How to win as a stepfamily*. New York: Dembner Books, 1982.

Wallerstein, J.S., & Kelly, J.B. *Surviving the breakup: How children and parents cope with divorce*. New York: Basic Books, 1980.

Weiss, R. *Marital separation*. New York: Basic Books, 1975.

Weiss, R.S. *Going it alone: The family life and social situation of the single parent*. New York: Basic Books, 1979.

Weltner, J.S. A structural approach to the single-parent family. *Family Process*, 1982, *21*, 203-210.

Whiteside, M.F. The role of explicit rule-making in the early stages of remarriage. In A.S. Gurman (Ed.), *Questions and answers in the practice of family therapy* (Vol. 2). New York: Brunner/Mazel, 1982.(a)

Whiteside, M.F. Remarriage: A family developmental process. *Journal of Marital and Family Therapy*, 1982, *8*, 59-68.(b)

8. The Timing of Symptoms and Critical Events in the Family Life Cycle

Froma Walsh, PhD
Associate Professor
School of Social Service Administration
The University of Chicago

Center for Family Studies/Family Institute of Chicago
Department of Psychiatry & Behavioral Sciences
Northwestern University Medical School
Chicago, Illinois

Family systems function in a temporal context as well as a social context. Attention to the systemic temporal context of symptoms adds an important dimension to the assessment and treatment of dysfunction, with application for all therapeutic approaches. The model of the three-generational family life cycle offers a guideline for taking into account the timing of symptoms and their relationship with past and current critical events that disrupt the family system. This paper identifies several common temporal linkages for therapists to be alert to in order to address family life cycle patterns associated with problem formation, maintenance, and resolution.

THE TEMPORAL CONTEXT OF DYSFUNCTION AND SYSTEMS-BASED THERAPIES

The temporal context of family interaction has been neglected in family systems theory and family therapy (McGoldrick & Walsh, 1983). An unfortunate dichotomy has arisen between so-called "historical and "ahistorical" models (Fisch, Weakland, & Segal, 1982; Madanes & Haley, 1977; Sluzki, 1981). Family therapy approaches termed historical, including psychodynamic, transgenerational, and Bowen models, have emphasized the uncovering and working through of past conflicts and losses in the family of origin that impair present relationships. Ahistorical approaches, including structural, strategic, and behavioral models, have restricted their focus to current, ongoing interactional patterns that maintain dysfunction.

Historical approaches rooted in psychoanalytic traditions are criticized for what is regarded as a genetic fallacy based on a linear-causal assumption of unidirectional influence. Since causation is viewed as a circular process of action and reaction in systems theory, the definition of an event as "the origin" of a problem is regarded as an arbitrary punctuation in an ongoing interactional stream of events. Moreover, a search for "the origin" of a problem can lead therapists to take a deterministic stance and to overemphasize the causal significance of events in the distant past—particularly events in early childhood—to the neglect of current interactional processes. In ahistorical approaches, historical information and events in the broader multigenerational family field tend to be discounted as either irrelevant or not useful to therapeutic change. Systems therapists most strongly influenced by cybernetic and communication theories conclude that the genetic question of why symptoms have developed is less useful to the process of change than the process question of how symptoms are maintained.

Such polarized positions on the value of historical information for therapy neglect and distort important temporal aspects of family process and of therapeutic change related to development and adaptation over the course of the life cycle. Both past and present should be taken into account. Recognition of the influence of the temporal context of symptoms need not imply linear causality any more than does recognition of the influence of the social context. The baby—in this case, a historical perspective—need not be discarded with the dirty bath water—a deterministic linear conception of history. Rather, as has been proposed by McGoldrick and Walsh (1983), a systemic view of history is needed to take into account the epigenesis of family process as the family moves forward in time over the generations and over the course of the life cycle.

From this perspective, life change events are examined not as linear causes, but as stressors that pose adaptive challenges for individuals and their families. Families do not simply react to life change events; they also actively influence the occurrence, course, and impact of events through their approach and response to them. Thus, the occurrence of critical events should be considered in terms of (1) the event as a stimulus for change; (2) the family's approach to the event; and (3) the family's response to the event, with immediate and long-term ramifications.

CRITICAL EVENT

The occurrence of major life change events stresses the entire family system, not only the individual members most directly affected. The impetus for change may come from within the system, at times of transition from one developmental stage to the next. Other pressures for change are externally imposed, such as forced retirement. Transition periods are characterized by a temporary disequilibrium in the family system, during which the family's stability and continuity may be threatened by demands for change and family members are likely to experience a sense of loss, confusion, and anxiety. Change events can be a stimulus either for successful adaptation or for dysfunction. A wide range of mental and physical disorders have been found to be associated with the occurrence of major change events, especially those involving important losses (Rahe, 1979). Problems are especially likely to be presented clinically at transition points in the family life cycle (Hadley, Jacob, Miliones, Caplan, & Spitz, 1974).

FAMILY APPROACH

A family's approach to an event affects its impact, and even, in some cases, the likelihood that the event will occur. Reiss (1982) demonstrated that each family's actions in a new situation are shaped by that family's paradigm, or basic premises for viewing and approaching life events. A family's paradigm is an enduring structure of shared beliefs, convictions, and assumptions about the social world that evolve from past experience. This set contributes to the family's perception of events, the meaning given to them, and expectations about their likely consequences. Catastrophic expectations (Feldman & Pinsof, 1982) can contribute to a systemic rigidity, or reluctance to change established patterns, and to symptoms that express the distress and may function to restore the homeostasis.

FAMILY RESPONSE

Families vary in their response to critical events, depending on their problem-solving style and their ability to maintain both integration and flexibility (Walsh, 1982). Major life events and life cycle transitions involve second order change, a reorganization of the family structure and alteration in the nature of relationships among family members (Hoffman, 1980). One member's change, such as the move away from home at the launching transition, alters not only that member's relationships with parents and siblings, but also other members' relationships with one another and the family as a whole. With the launching of the last child, an entire reorganization of the family takes place, as parents must shift from triad to dyad, and from a two-generation household to a couple unit.

A family's approach and response to an event are influenced both by its sociocultural context and by its past experience over many generations. The significance of a particular life event, the normative timing of its occurrence, and the rituals that mark it vary with different cultures and ethnic groups (McGoldrick, Pearce, & Giordano, 1982). Expectations and reactions to events are largely influenced by social norms, the perceptions of expectable events in the typical life cycle of average families in the dominant society (Walsh, 1983). Events perceived as occurring "on time" with people's expectations about the normal life cycle are less stressful and more easily adjusted to than events that occur "off time," meaning earlier or later than the norm, or at an atypical point in the life cycle (Neugarten, 1970). For example, adjustment to widowhood is more difficult for younger widows than for older widows; in contrast, adjustment to divorce tends to be more problematic for older adults. The death of a child is generally much more traumatic for a family than is the death of an elderly family member who has lived a full life. Adaptation is also likely to be more difficult when the timing of life cycle transitions in a subculture differs from that of such transitions in the dominant society (Falicov & Karrer, 1980).

Each family's own past also influences its approach and response to events. The legacy of past experience extends over at least three generations and includes not only the past events themselves, but also the myths surrounding them (Carter & McGoldrick, 1980). It also includes the family relational patterns that took shape or shifted at those nodal points in time and have persisted to the present or may be reactivated by a current event. Family life cycle transitions are especially likely to be influenced by past experience, since each generation has had to confront the challenges of passage through successive stages. Even though the particular circumstances of life transitions by previous generations may have been quite different from present circumstances at the same transition one or more generations later, the current event is likely to evoke feelings and reactions—both conscious and unconscious—associated with the same transition point in the past. Thus, the birth of a child is likely to reactivate for both parents feelings and selective memories of their own infancy and the parenting they received. The style and ability of a family to confront and to master current life cycle challenges is, therefore, greatly influenced by the manner and ability of past generations to handle the same transition point. In fact, many families function rather well until they reach a critical point in the life cycle at which complications had arisen a generation earlier. Thus, it is imperative to identify past critical events that intersect with current transition points in order to address related concerns in the current life cycle passage (Carter, 1978; McGoldrick & Walsh, 1983).

Just as life events that occur "off time" in relation to normative expectations are likely to generate more stress, so too will such "off time" events be more likely to hold impact for the next generation at the same moment in life cycle passage. A survey of the normal (nonclinical) population (Neugarten, 1970) found a strong correlation between the age at which individuals expected they would die and the age at death of their deceased parents. Symptoms are often presented in a family at the time a member reaches the age at which his or her parent—or counterpart, such as a spouse's parent—died, particularly when the parent died earlier than would normally be expected. For example, one man who had a reputation for outstanding achievement throughout adulthood suddenly became dysfunctional and physically self-destructive (failing to follow medical orders for recovery from surgery) during the year of his 48th birthday, the age at which his father had died. At such times, an entire family may shift its organization and communication patterns to protect the survival of the member identified with past events, and anxiety may be deflected to another member who is considered less vulnerable. Thus, in addition to the immediate interactional context of the symptom bearers it is important to look to the temporal patterns in the broader three-generational field.

In summary, a systems perspective of history takes into account the impact of critical events that disrupt the family, as well as the family's approach and response to the events. This includes the long-term legacy for future generations, particularly as they reach the same life cycle transition. Patterns of approach and response to events are beyond the scope of this paper and are considered more fully elsewhere (McGoldrick and Walsh, 1983). The point to be underscored here is that families do, in fact, punctuate the stream of their experience by significant events over the course of the life cycle, especially those events that have disrupted—or threaten to disrupt—their lives. Thus, it is imperative for clinicians to note the timing of symptoms. The question ''Why now?'' can be as important to the therapy as the question ''How now?'' In other words not only the process or mechanisms by which symptoms are maintained but also the life cycle issues associated with the specific timing of symptoms require attention.

TIMING OF SYMPTOMS AND LIFE CYCLE EVENTS

As a part of any clinical assessment, whether for emotional, behavioral, or physical problems, it is recommended that the timing of onset and exacerbation of symptoms (e.g., the point at which treatment was sought or hospitalization required) be noted in relation to significant life events in the three-generational family field. This should include the tracking of recent events, over the past year, and impending events, over the coming year. Both major transitions to a new stage in the life cycle and single events of particular import to the family should be noted. Events marking loss, such as death, launching, separation, and divorce tend to be particularly stressful for families. Other events that are typically anticipated eagerly, such as marriage, birth of the first child, and remarriage, are also stressful because of the complications of reorganization. While the developmental tasks associated with various events differ, it should be noted that all major transitions involve both loss and reorganization.

Past nodal events in the three-generational family field that may have a bearing on the family's present dilemma should also be tracked. If time permits, inquiry might include an evolutionary, sequential reconstruction of major events and turning points in the parents' courtship, the nuclear family, and the families of origin. A more limited, focused inquiry should include particular attention to the following moments in time:

1. past events at the same point in the life cycle, a generation earlier, as the family's current stage or transition
2. events that occurred when the parent(s) of a symptom bearer was at the same age as the identified patient's age at onset or exacerbation of symptoms
3. events that concurred with a major developmental transition involving the identified patient, particularly at the time of birth

These moments in the family's current and past life cycle passage are commonly linked with symptoms and symptom maintenance in family systems. The following case examples illustrate the potential linkages that contribute to the timing of symptoms and to their resolution.

Symptom Concurrence with Nodal Event

At the time treatment is requested—either the onset of acute symptoms or the severe exacerbation of a chronic condition—it is important to determine whether there are concurrent change events in the family field that make this particular time more stressful than usual. It is crucial to inquire beyond the direct stress on the individual symptom bearer and to determine if there is stress on other parts of the system or on the system as a whole.

> In one family, a suicide attempt was made by a 14-year-old daughter on the same night as her father's third job loss that year. Job loss had particular meaning in that family; both parents had grown up in fragmented families forced to exist on welfare, and a cornerstone of their marital vows had been the determination to provide for their children in order to hold their family together.

A major transition to a new stage in the family life cycle poses demands for second order change, involving structural reorganization and alterations in the nature and rules of relationships (Hoffman, 1980). Shifts required at the time the first child is born and at the time the last child is launched are especially stressful. Other transitions disrupt established patterns and involve losses as well as gains. At retirement, for example, the spouse may become symptomatic with depression or anxiety related to shifts in the marital relationship, changes in patterns of daily life, and concerns about the future (Walsh, 1980).

Symptoms in one subsystem may be connected to major transitions in other parts of the system.

> The parents of an adolescent boy presented concerns that their son's behavior was out of control. At the same time, a grandparent in the family was losing control to a debilitating illness. The parents felt an obligation to care for the grandparent, yet an inability to control or manage the situation. As the parents focused their concerns on whether their son would need to be institutionalized, they faced the question of institutionalization of the aging parent; they were unable to discuss or deal with it, however, because of their conflicting feelings about their responsibilities to their parents and communication blockages in the marriage. Those issues needed immediate attention in therapy (Walsh, 1980).

Therapists attending to ongoing interactional patterns should not assume that a long-standing conflictual marital style is the problem to be resolved when the problem may be a recent or impending change disrupting that pattern. Research on normal families has found that no particular style of interaction is inherently pathogenic or symptom producing (Walsh, 1982). Even when an interactional pattern has been chronically unsatisfying or dysfunctional for members, it may not be the impetus for seeking treatment at the present time. Clinicians' overattention to ongoing, repetitive interactional cycles may distract them from immediate concerns relating to recent or impending change.

> A man was brought to a hospital emergency room following a suicide attempt. When asked about his marriage, he described a nightly ritual throughout his marriage whereby he would undress and lay out his belt at bedtime, and his wife would chase him around the house beating him with the belt. The intake worker assumed that what he judged to be a rather bizarre and destructive pattern had finally driven the poor man to attempt to take his life to escape. The supervisor pressed the worker to find out what had brought the man to that point at that particular time when he had never before sought help or complained of his situation. The worker then learned that the man's wife had just threatened to leave him.

In assessing the family context of a presenting problem, therapists must think of the family as evolving, moving forward in time. Interactional patterns observed in an interview are only a cross-sectional view of the family at a single moment in time. It is important to understand the direction in which a family is headed, as well as the direction from which it is emerging.

A father requested help for problems with his elder son's oppositional behavior with him. The household consisted of the father and his two sons, for whom he was custodial parent. Family therapy was begun, focusing on the triadic interactional patterns surrounding the father-son conflicts. When no progress had been made after several sessions, a consultant was called in; the consultant inquired about recent and impending changes in the family. When the consultant asked how the parents' divorce had occurred a year earlier and how it had changed their family, it bacame clear that the breakup of the family was still acutely painful for all members and that relationships and contact with the mother were confused and highly conflictual. An immediate precipitant to the escalation of conflict between the father and son was the mother's recent announcement of remarriage. Immediately thereafter, the father felt under sudden pressure from his girlfriend to remarry also, but he was unable either to commit himself or to end the relationship. The sons were reluctant to "replace" the mother. Paralyzed at this decision-point, the family became preoccupied by the escalating father-son conflicts. A crucial therapeutic task was to help the family with the sequence of transitions from an intact family to a one-parent household and co-parenting arrangements to consideration of becoming a remarried family unit. This involved making connections between the recent and impending transitions and multiple triangles in which the father-son conflict was embedded.

Symptom at Transgenerational Anniversary: Same Transition

The occurrence of symptoms is often found to coincide with complications in past generations at the same point of transition in the life cycle, especially if loss was involved.

A family was referred for therapy following the drug overdose of their 22-year-old son on the eve of his wedding. The mother acknowledged that it was much harder for her to have this son (her namesake) leave home and marry than it had been when his elder siblings had left home, although she could not say—nor could others—what made his leaving special. The consultant suggested that the therapist ask the parents when and how they had left home. The mother burst into tears in response, reporting that 6 months after she had left home to marry, her father had died suddenly of a heart attack. Her words were "It feels the same. I don't know why but it feels the same as my son's leaving makes me feel."

When a contextual replication takes place, feelings and events in the present are linked to those in the past. It may be useful to make covert associations overt and then to differentiate the two experiences. Here a therapeutic choice point is presented. A psychodynamically oriented therapist might choose to focus more extensively on the past loss and work toward its resolution. A therapist with a structural or strategic orientation might instead limit intervention to unblocking the current interactional impasse and use the linkage to address the current life cycle transition as an opportunity to "do it differently" from the past experience. Rituals might be prescribed to mark this event and to facilitate the family developmental transition.

Symptom at Transgenerational Anniversary: Same Age

A transgenerational linkage may be more specifically focused on age; symptoms may occur in the child when he or she reaches the age of the parent at the time of a stressful event. An example has been given of a man who became self-destructive when he reached the age at which his father had died prematurely. Symptoms are likely to be even more severe when an emotional and physical cutoff from the past has occurred and communication about linkages has been forbidden.

An 18-year-old boy was hospitalized for an acute psychotic reaction that occurred on a summer vacation in Europe. The father had been interred in a concentration camp in Germany at the age of 18, at which time he had lost contact permanently with both parents and had witnessed the shooting of his brother. He survived the war, came to the United States, and married. His wife told how, on their first date, she had asked about the camp numbers on his arm, and seeing him so visibly shaken, had decided never to mention the past again. As the children grew up, no one ever discussed the father's past, although the numbers on his arm were a constant reminder. When the son reached his 18th birthday, the father gave him a trip to Europe as a birthday present. While there, the son became profoundly depressed, broke the rule of silence, and wrote home that he knew what had happened to his father at the same age and, therefore, could not enjoy a holiday at the same time and place. His parents did not reply; he suffered a breakdown that brought him home.

In family therapy, communication was opened on the linkage of past and present. Although everyone had been considerate of the father's feelings over the years to spare him further pain, it was agreed that this was no longer necessary, as the father was not as vulnerable as he had been earlier in his life. On case follow-up a year later, it was learned that the son was doing well in college and, incidentally, majoring in Communications. The family also reported that the mother and father had made a trip to the father's native village in Poland, which had been an important experience for them both.

Events Concurrent with Developmental Transition of Symptom Bearer: Birth

It is useful to examine the specific time around the birth of an identified patient to determine whether concurrent events were linked with the birth of that particular child. The death of a significant family member around the time of the birth may have special relevance. The death of a child—an unexpected loss—is a particularly painful event. In a high proportion of families, such a loss is followed by divorce. In other families, a sibling may serve a special replacement function for the family; frequently this role is assigned to another child conceived within months of the loss or anticipated loss. While such a triangulation process may stabilize the system and compensate for the loss, it may have long-term pathological consequences if the process has blocked mourning and interferes with the child's differentiation.

A 12-year-old boy attempted suicide and was hospitalized. The boy and his family made no mention of an older brother until the therapist's inquiries about the family system elicited the information that the boy was born six months before the death of his brother, who had been hospitalized for rheumatic fever at the age of 12. He grew up believing himself to be the reincarnation of his dead brother sent by God to make his family happy again. The father, who could not remember the date or events surrounding the death, wished to remember his first son "as if he were still alive." The boy cultivated his appearance to resemble photos of his dead brother and developed similar behavioral and emotional styles. Only when asked about his brother did the boy state that he attempted suicide "to join his 12-year-old brother in heaven." The timing of the attempt also corresponded with the boy's growth spurt at the onset of puberty and his concern that he was changing from the way he was "supposed" to look. Therapy focused on enabling the boy and his family to relinquish his surrogate position and to move forward with tasks of differentiation appropriate to the developmental transition into adolescence.

Again, it is crucial to inspect the three-generational family field, particularly for a death in the grandparent generation that is concurrent with the birth of the child who is later symptomatic. Independent studies by McGoldrick Orfanidis and Walsh (Walsh, 1978) found that over 40% of schizophrenic patients had been born within 2 years of a grandparent death; in other words, either the mother or the father had lost a parent at the time of conception and birth of that child. The death/birth concurrence was significantly greater than that for siblings in the same families. Concurrence was also significantly more frequent for schizophrenics than for other severely disturbed nonschizophrenic patients, although concurrence did occur in over 20% of those cases as well. Concurrence was greater for *both* patient groups than for the nonclinical normal population (around 8% death/birth concurrence). In sum, the concurrence of events—without consideration of approach or response to those events—distinguished severely dysfunctional from normal families.

Such findings support the hypothesis of Mueller and McGoldrick Orfanidis (1976) that the schizophrenic patient serves a special replacement function, stabilizing the family by replacing the lost parent-grandparent relationship. The rigid pattern is disrupted by attempted separation when the schizophrenic reaches the normal launching point in young adulthood, the time when the first schizophrenic breakdown most often occurs. Some family therapists, notably Haley (1980), have concentrated on a dysfunctional young adult's coalition and function vis a vis the parents' marital relationship, failing to take into account other possible functions of symptoms in the three-generational system. Attention to a past loss and the family's reorganizational response is necessary in order to recognize this aspect of the protective function of the patient's symptoms and the nature of the family impasse at the launching transition.

CONCLUSION

Tracking significant events in the three-generational family life cycle provides valuable information for the assessment of dysfunction and the formulation of treatment objectives. It is most useful to note linkages between the timing of symptoms and both current and past critical events which disrupted—or threaten to disrupt—the family system. A genogram and a family time line are useful tools for assessment of temporal patterns, particularly in ordering and clarifying information of potential relevance to presenting problems and problem resolution. Such diagrams are especially helpful with severely dysfunctional families, in which vague or fragmented accounts blur or distort temporal linkages and symptoms appear to be irrational and dissociated from any contextual meaning. The identification of associated nodal events points to life cycle issues in which symptoms may be embedded so that therapy can address them.

Various approaches to therapy, with differing objectives, strategies, and techniques, may utilize such information differently. A psychodynamically oriented or Bowenian approach might choose to focus extensively and intensively on resolution of past issues, such as unresolved mourning. A structural or strategic approach might instead limit therapeutic intervention to unblocking the immediate impasse, such as addressing a current life cycle transition. The therapeutic choice involves decisions about how much emphasis is given to the past or to the present in the change process. An integrative approach might begin with the present and draw on relevant past experience when a current impasse is not readily resolved. Regardless of the therapeutic approach, an important dimension is added to therapy when life cycle issues that link past, present, and future for a family are taken into account. Attention to the timing of critical events sheds light on pertinent life cycle issues.

REFERENCES

Carter, E. Transgenerational scripts and nuclear family stress. In R. Sager (Ed.), *Georgetown family symposium: 1975-76*. Washington, DC: Georgetown University, 1978.

Carter, E., & McGoldrick, M. *The family life cycle: A framework for family therapy*. New York: Gardner Press, 1980.

Falicov, C., & Karrer, B. Cultural variations in the normal family life cycle: The Mexican-American family. In E. Carter & M. McGoldrick (Eds.), *The family life cycle: A framework for family therapy*. New York: Gardner Press, 1980.

Feldman, L., & Pinsof, W. Problem maintenance in family systems: An integrative model. *Journal of Marital and Family Therapy*, 1982, *8*, 295-308.

Fisch, R., Weakland, J., & Segal, L. *The tactics of change*. San Francisco: Jossey Bass, 1982.

Hadley, T., Jacob, T., Miliones, J., Caplan, J., & Spitz, D. The relationship between family developmental crisis and the appearance of symptoms in a family member. *Family Process*, 1974, *13*, 207-214.

Haley, J. *Leaving home*. New York: McGraw-Hill, 1980.

Hoffman, L. The family life cycle and discontinuous change. In E. Carter & M. McGoldrick (Eds.), *The family life cycle: A framework for family therapy*. New York: Gardner Press, 1980.

Madanes, C., & Haley, J. Dimensions of family therapy. *Journal of Nervous and Mental Disease*, 1977, *165*, 88-98.

McGoldrick, M., Pearce, J., & Giordano, J. *Ethnicity and family therapy*. New York: Guilford Press, 1982.

McGoldrick, M., & Walsh, F. A systemic view of family history and loss. In M. Aronson & L. Wolberg (Eds.), *Group and family therapy 1983*. New York: Brunner/Mazel, 1983.

Mueller, P., & McGoldrick Orfanidis, M. A method of co-therapy for schizophrenic families. *Family Process*, 1976, *15*, 179-192.

Neugarten, B. Dynamics of transition of middle age to old age: Adaptation and the life cycle. *Journal of Geriatric Psychiatry*, 1970, *4*. 71-87.

Rahe, R. Life change events and mental illness: An overview. *Journal of Human Stress*, 1979, *5*, 2-10.

Reiss, D. *The family's construction of reality*. Cambridge, Mass: Harvard University Press, 1982.

Sluzki, C. Process of symptom production and patterns of symptom maintenance. *Journal of Marital and Family Therapy*, 1981, *7*, 273-280.

Walsh, F. The family in later life. In E. Carter & M. McGoldrick (Eds.), *The family life cycle: A framework for family therapy*. New York: Gardner Press, 1980.

Walsh, F. Conceptualizations of normal family functioning. In F. Walsh (Ed.), *Normal family processes*. New York: Guilford Press, 1982.

Walsh, F. Normal family ideologies: Myths and realities. In C. Falicov (Ed.), *Cultural dimensions of family therapy*. Rockville, MD: Aspen Systems Corporation, 1983.

Walsh, F. Concurrent grandparent death and birth of schizophrenic offspring: An intriguing finding. *Family Process*, 1978, *4*, 457-464.

9. The Therapist's New Role: Training Families for Healthy Survival

Virginia Morgan McFadden, MSW

George Doub, MFCC
Eastfield Children's Center
Campbell, California

THE FIELD OF FAMILY THERAPY IS EXPERIENCING A SHIFT OF FOCUS from pathological states to healthy states, and from individual interventions to systemic interventions. Armed with new skills and new theoretical frameworks for addressing family needs, today's family therapist has an opportunity to move from the role of pathologist to the role of consultant, and from the role of therapist to the role of trainer. Family therapists interested in a competency-based model are expanding their arena of influence beyond mental health agencies and into the community.

We have developed a course to help large groups of families develop skills for healthy living. The course is based on a "family wellness" model that uses layman's language and focuses on competence, providing the trainers and the participants with a framework of health. Courses such as this one not only will elicit more focused referrals to the mental health system, but also will ultimately reduce the number of families who need therapy, drug treatment, or crisis intervention.

THEORETICAL FRAMEWORK

Some of the difficulty experienced by families is due to lack of information, lack of a sufficiently complex family organization, and lack of support from other families. When people are given information about healthy family dynamics, a context for the development and practice of new family rules, and support from their family members and community, they can learn to live together more productively and enjoyably. Three main sources contributed to the design of this course: family life cycle theory, family systems theory, and structural family therapy.

Problems are viewed as derailments from normal development in the family life cycle. Stress is expected as families move from one stage of development to the next and new structures must be created to accommodate newly emerging family needs. Family members already conditioned to look for their mistakes must slowly reorganize to develop constructive coping patterns. Helping families step back and look at the larger time frame of their life cycle is particularly useful in promoting realignments with extended family members. Many grandparents and grown children who attend the course renegotiate their status with other family members and open discussion about their mutual needs.

Two fundamental principles of this course come from systems theory. The first, *interrelatedness,* states that change in any one member both affects and is affected by change in any other. Thus, cause for any behavior is circular, stemming from all family members, and is never isolated in an individual. Systems theory also teaches that a family must have not only stability but also adaptability—the ability to reorganize as it moves from one stage of development to another.

Specific views of normal family functioning are drawn primarily from structural family therapy, developed by Minuchin (1974), who maintained that a healthy family is one that has a structure appropriate to its needs. This structure varies according to the family's needs; its effectiveness depends on its responsiveness to the evolving needs of all family members for both autonomy and belonging. Structural family therapy also provides the concepts of hierarchy and boundaries for evaluating and teaching about healthy family organization.

METHODS

This approach is unique in its training format. While both didactic and experiential training techniques are used in the course, the main emphasis is on experiential methods. Most family therapists are well equipped to utilize therapeutic strategies for teaching family survival skills. Underlying the process are the clearly stated and modeled rules for trainers: (1) the trainers, as the consultants in family systems, and the families, as those who know their own needs, must work together; and (2) the trainers are in charge of creating an environment that improves families' abilities to foster health among members.

Role Play/Enactments

Recreating in the session what a family actually does and what it can do to stay healthy is the central tool of teaching the rules for family survival. Therapists know the value of doing rather than talking. Every opportunity is taken to engage the audience and to act out their questions and problems in an environment that provides support for different ways of doing things. Families learn new behaviors by observing models and by practicing them. Three variations on role play are used:

1. trainer scene. The trainers plan the content, structure the situation, and play the parts. This allows for the most control and is the least threatening to the participants. It is used to elicit interest, questions, and comments.

2. trainer-directed scene. The content and the situation are assigned, and participants are recruited to play the parts. The trainer can highlight chosen content while broadening participant involvement.
3. audience scene. The dramatization is based on the issues or questions of participants and enacted by them. The trainer must be highly skilled to maintain the focus on education, as the combination of personal issues and willing participants can lead to a therapy session rather than a lesson based on a personal vignette. The correct balance is best maintained by periodically acknowledging the audience through asides to them, creating stop-actions to point out the relationship between events in the dramatization and the material being taught, and summarizing with the role play participants the unique application of a healthy family pattern to their personal situation.

In all of the models for role play, the trainers call on a variety of related skills—coaching, doubling, asides, position, movement, instruction, stop-action, and audience participation.

The typical and most effective prelude to this learning "dance" is a question from the audience.

> What if your daughter doesn't listen to you because you're her father and not her mother, and she isn't living with you most of the time?

This father would be invited to come up in front of the group and play himself, with coaching, so that he can talk sense to his angry daughter, played by the other trainer. In some cases, a second member of the same family or another participant is invited up: "We need an angry daughter; this is a chance to play out the other side for most of you parents." One trainer stands near the father to coach him. The other trainer, if he or she is not playing the part of the daughter, coaches the person who is. Either trainer may stop action to ask the players if they are getting what they wanted or if what they are doing is working. Trainers also offer the players an alternate word and behavior: "Try walking over and standing next to her. She needs to know that you are more than just words." Trainers double or act as alter egos for participants to demonstrate a way to proceed. Often while in role, the trainers make comments to the audience to offer another perspective for dealing with the issues raised or to point out a transactional pattern.

Two other variations often occur in role play. If the person who asks a question is reluctant to play out the scene, another person may be invited to stand in for that person. The action is stopped periodically to ask the initiator of the question if the situation is being portrayed accurately. If the person who asks a question will play the part only from the audience, another variation may be used: the trainer goes to the person's seat and either coaches or acts out the other side from there.

Each role play is ended at a point of success for the main actor. The ending is not always happy, but the person has applied a rule for healthy living and has been able to see the results in this first practice session. The trainers then underline the lesson and publicly acknowledge the actor's success. This support is reinforced at each succeeding session for those who report changed behavior and for those who participate in role play. The audience is helped to integrate the experience through a dialogue initiated by their questions and comments.

Rules for Change

To maximize the possibility for change—change from having ineffective family structures to having healthy family structures, change from being observers to being participants, change from being tired parents to being active parents—the course offers clear, simple rules and encourages behavioral transformation in a way that makes the theory practical and personal. The environment provides a safe and supportive arena in which participants are challenged to try out new behaviors. Each rule of healthy living is presented visually, discussed, and demonstrated before the participants are asked to practice it.

The "doing" is emphasized, supported, and even celebrated by the group. The possible steps to particular changes are explained in behaviorally measurable terms so that the participants can see when they have followed a rule, hear the results, and feel the difference. The transformation of one member of the group may produce other changes, and a change that would be unnoticed by a trainer may be noticed and appreciated by the group participants.

Audio/Visual Tools

Use of a large pad allows for simple visual presentations, summaries, and the highlighting of particular issues. Excerpts from videotapes of prior courses on particular issues are also effective teaching aides. Handouts that summarize the rules and some brief notes on each rule should be provided at the beginning of each session.

Audience Interaction

The course is designed to give participants a heightened sense of community with other families. Small group activities, which are very well received by the audience, are used in the sessions on couples and families with other families. Mixing males and females in the groups and providing focused discussion questions guarantees that experiences will be shared and the session rules supported.

STYLE

The foundations of the course are a solid content and proved trainer skills, but the magic that transforms these basics into a living experience lies in the personal style of the trainers. Two different people, each with individual skills and particular ways of relating to others, become a third entity, blending their attributes and their abilities to engage various members of the group. The dance between trainers and participants is modeled by the dance of the two trainers as they build on each other's personality and style.

Our particular team was formed over 5 years ago and now represents over 35 years of teaching, counseling, and training experience. As a male-female team with a variety of life experiences, we have many points of contact with the audience. One of us is a married Latino with a 12-year-old child at home; the other has been a single parent for the past 9 years, after 13 years of marriage, and has two grown children. We draw from our own family experiences in our training.

As a training team, we model the basic rule for families. We have a plan, stay in charge (at least one of us stays in charge, while the other may become more playful, rest, or observe), stick together, and enjoy our work. Keeping the rules helps us to enjoy the training. Being playful gives us the perspective and creative edge to engage individuals and the group. In the 5 years we have conducted training sessions together, we have developed an easy trust in each other that allows us to work cooperatively. The model of a couple working together is in itself powerful. We demonstrate the subtle, subjective parts of family life that cannot be transmitted in words. Blending training skills with teamwork creates a powerful tool for teaching survival skills to families.

The rationale for co-trainers is the same as that for co-therapists. When there is more than one trainer, each has an opportunity to observe while the other teaches, responds, or participates in role play. The complexity of audience problems, interruptions, and personalities is matched by the diversity of skills and the energy in the trainers. The male-female team makes it possible to model traditional family interactions, demonstrating in a credible fashion the problems and styles of male and female participants. The male-female team also permits each trainer to connect consciously with various members of the audience and the issues that concern them.

To conduct this course successfully requires a trust in the unknown. Each trainer brings to the course a personal style, and each group of people attending is unique. The course content, presented by skilled and flexible trainers, will in all likelihood provide both trainers and participants with the opportunity to take risks, experiment, play, and learn.

RECRUITMENT AND FUNDING

The course, divided into five 2-hour evening sessions, is designed for an audience of 25 to 150 people. People of all ages are encouraged to attend the entire course or any individual sessions they choose, except the one on couples, which is open only to adults. People may attend as individuals or as families.

We have presented the course five times in Santa Cruz County, California: in a farming area, where it was conducted in Spanish and English; in a working class neighborhood with many single mothers; in an upper middle-class suburban high school; in a mountain town with a high incidence of chemical dependency in teen-agers; and in a resort town with a wide variety of people. The first course required extensive recruiting through posters, personal telephoning, newspaper articles, and public service announcements on radio and TV. An average of only 40 people attended. The second course also required recruitment efforts. Once it had begun, however, people invited friends, who invited friends, and the audience size became unmanageable. Ideally, questions and responses are audible without a microphone. The need for the course was reemphasized in each session as the audience continued to grow. Two reporters came for one session to spend 10 or 15 minutes; they stayed the entire session and wrote a full-page article with pictures for the local press. The course sells itself.

Funding was provided by the Family Wellness Project of Wingspread, a nonprofit health services center directed by Josette Mondanaro, M.D. Because this program was supported by a grant from the California Department of Alcohol and Drug Programs, we were able to offer the course free of charge, including child care, informational handouts, and coffee. Many foundations and even government grants are turning to prevention in an effort to provide support for families. At least six major national foundations are currently emphasizing family wellness or support for parents and families.

THE COURSE CONTENT: SURVIVAL SKILLS FOR HEALTHY FAMILIES

The general format is the same for each of the sessions:

1. opening scene
2. introduction and review
3. presentation of the rules
4. skill development through application of the rules
5. summary
6. evaluation

Each session begins with a 3- to 5-minute role play by the trainers. This encapsulates the topic for the evening, engages people's interest, and introduces the personalities of the instructors. The best opening scene role plays are the ones that emerge from the trainers' personal or professional experience. After the first session, the trainers use the introductions to guide the participants through a verbal review of what they learned in the previous sessions and ask for examples of how people have applied their new knowledge to their lives. Then the rules to be discussed at the session are presented, and the participants are given an opportunity to practice using them.

The content of the session is summarized at the end of each evening, and people are reminded that this is only one-fifth of what families need to do to ensure the health of their members. Also at the end of each session, the audience is asked to fill out a simple four-question evaluation form:

1. What did you like about this session?
2. What would you change?
3. What do you want to learn from this session?
4. What would you like other classes on?

These evaluations are used to assess what was effective, what needs to be changed, and what other issues should be discussed. Not only do we read the evaluations after each session, but also we tell the audience that this feedback is helping to shape the course. We also schedule a weekly time to evaluate the course. Videotapes are extremely useful for this; even without them, however, it is beneficial to set aside a specific time to evaluate the teaching style, the techniques used, the audience participation, and the course content.

Week 1: How to Survive as a Parent in a Healthy Family

Ginny: George! *(calls in a loud voice to George, who is off to the side)* I think there are a few things we need to clear up about the way you talked to Shannon this morning. You were just too insensitive.

George: *(aside to audience, as walks to front)* Here we go again. All I ever get is complaints and "shoulds." *(to Ginny)* Yes, Ginny, I never seem to do anything right for *your* daughter. What's wrong now?

Ginny: You need to be more sensitive to her. She is 12 and very sensitive about how she looks and what she wears. She doesn't need you to comment on her complexion and her hairdo just before she goes to school. *(aside)* I wish he'd be less critical of me, too.

George: Look, you have always favored Shannon just because she is yours. You baby her and pick on Roger. He never has the right to be late, take a long time in the bathroom, or anything.

Ginny: Well, maybe I do give Shannon a little more slack . . . but we could work this out together if you were willing to *talk* about how we raise our kids instead of coming in and yelling orders to everyone, including me.

George: OK, I'm willing to work this out; but not in front of all these people. Let's take a half hour tonight after the course.

Both: *(to audience)* Welcome to Survival Skills for Healthy Families.

Ginny: For the next five weeks George and I will be looking with you at families. We hope to give you some expanded ways to look at your own families and time to talk with one another about what makes your family work better, rather than what hurts it. Maybe we can start by introducing ourselves.

The first evening, the trainers introduce themselves, using both personal and professional credentials. Members of the audience are welcomed and

nvited to say what they hope to gain by attending. A written outline of the
entire series is distributed. The members of the audience are encouraged to
make a contract with themselves to attend and participate in all five sessions.

The trainers define a family as a unit of two or more people who are
sharing a household and consider themselves a family. The job of a family is
to provide for the physical safety and the ongoing personal development of
all its members. The audience is reminded that the rules to be presented are
guidelines for many types of healthy families, e.g., two-parent and single-
parent families, homosexual couples, and shared households of unrelated
adults and children.

As a final part of the initial introduction, the course objectives are stated.
At the end of the course, participants will

1. be able to identify the basic rules common to healthy families
2. have had opportunities to practice the rules during the sessions, with
   coaching from the trainers
3. have met with other families and discussed ways to cope with common
   family problems

The rules presented in the first session are as follows:

1. Make rules.
2. Stay in charge.
3. Stick together.
4. Make room to play with your children.
5. Change with the times.

Parents need to be challenged to take on the rights of parenthood when
they assume the responsibilities. We emphasize that rules of behavior are the
skeleton or structure of all families' lives; they help to hold a family together
by providing a tangible structure that allows for predictability and fun. Some
rules are made formally and acknowledged, e.g., go to church on Sundays
and do not watch TV on school nights. Some rules are made informally and
rarely acknowledged; never ask Mom why she cries in the night and do not
cry when your feelings are hurt. Whatever the constellation of rules, they
collectively comprise the identity of a family.

We illustrate the extremes in family rule structures. A brief family scene
is enacted with one parent advocating a lack of structure and the other parent
advocating excessive organization.

Mother: I have to leave for my meeting now. Please see to it that David is in bed by 6:30.

Father: 6:30! Why?

Mother: *(sternly, like a drill sergeant)* We changed the schedule just last week; he's to be down for breakfast by 7:45, dressed and ready to leave for school. And would you believe, he ambled down this morning at 7:55 and almost missed his bus!

Father: You and your schedules! Can't you just create some free space in our house? Mellow out! David's not the kind of kid who can be caged in—he's like me, a free spirit.

Reminding parents that no one knows their family needs better than they do, we teach parents to be the prime designers of the rules that govern their family life. Parents who are skeptical of the emphasis on rules will question this advice. We caution them that, if they do not provide structure by making rules, someone else will. A scene is used to demonstrate parents' most common replacements—their own parents or their children.

Mother: Your mother spoils Yolanda every time we leave her there. She gives her anything she wants, and then Yolanda comes home demanding the same queenly treatment here.

Father: My mother means well. Besides, she's doing us a favor. She said it was better for Yolanda to be with her while you're working than with a babysitter.

Mother: I was never sure that was a good idea. She does help out, but I'm not happy about Yolanda's bossy behavior since she's been staying there.

Father: Ah, relax. My mother knows how to raise a child. Look at me! I don't like Yolanda being bossy either, but what else can we do?

Mother: Maybe we're just worrying about nothing.

Father: Yeah, it's a stage Yolanda will outgrow. Incidentally, Mom called yesterday. She wants you to buy Yolanda some new shoes. She's taking her to a party on Thursday.

By this point in the session, the need for the parent to stay in charge can usually be demonstrated rather than discussed. Chris, a single mother with two teen-aged sons, asks what to do when they refuse to listen. Chris is invited to come up front and enact her situation. In this case, one trainer plays her son, taking cues from Chris on how to play him, and the other stands near Chris, prepared to coach.

Chris:	Adam, I want you to clean up those dishes you left in the sink.
Adam:	*(continues to read)*
Chris:	*(sighs)* Why won't you listen to me?
Adam:	*(reads)*
Chris:	How can you expect me to take care of you all the time? You've never done your share.
Trainer to Chris:	Are you getting what you want?
Chris:	No, he's not listening, he's . . .
Trainer:	OK, hold on a minute. State the rule again, and nothing else.
Chris:	Adam, clean up the dishes.
Adam:	Can't you see I'm doing my homework?
Chris:	*(turns to trainer)* See, he's impossible!
Trainer:	Stay with it; you're doing fine. Just say what he is to do. He doesn't have to like it. You just stay in charge.
Chris:	I want the dishes done by 6 o'clock.
Adam:	Why can't you do them?
Chris:	No, . . . *(hesitates, about to speak)*
Trainer:	Now walk away.

Chris does so, and the audience applauds. The debriefing underlines the need for parents to stay focused and expect resistance as they set rules.

The first two rules reinforce the need for hierarchy in a family. The third, stick together, introduces the nature of triads into the discussion. Through a series of role plays, parents are helped to recognize how, if they fail to cooperate with one another, their child or their parents and siblings can come between them to the detriment of everyone.

Child:	*(crying)* Mom, I don't want to go out trick or treating.
Dad:	Come on, stop crying, you don't have to be afraid of anything. We'll have a good time.
Mom:	Doug, you're scaring him. Remember he's just 4 years old and can't always act grown up.

Dad: He'll have a good time. He's just a little scared from going to that house last year where they had the scary music and the monster costumes. He has to get over this crying business, and you've got to help me with it. You baby him.

Mom: Well, I wouldn't have to protect him if you would remember his age and not push him so hard.

Child: (whining) Mom, can I have some ice cream?

Dad: See, I can't stand that whining he does with you.

Mom: Not now, Bill, your father and I are talking.

Child: But, Mom, I don't have to go trick or treating, do I?

Mom: I don't have an answer for you yet. Your dad and I are deciding.

Dad: Thanks, it's easier for me to lighten up on him when you help make him listen.

Mom: You're welcome. I know what you mean. It's easier for me to set limits on him when I know you'll take it easier on him, too.

Both abuse and neglect are signs of a parent's desperation and lack of control. In a healthy family, when one person is unable to maintain control and establish appropriate rules, another will seek help for that person and for the family. Healthy parents ask for help when they need it.

Healthy divorced and blended families develop and maintain workable co-parenting relationships. In the following role play, the father elicits support from his new spouse.

Stepmother: Tell your son to stop talking back to me.

Father: He's just having a hard time. He misses his mother.

Stepmother: That's no reason for him to be rude to me.

Father: We'd better sit down and figure out how to handle him, or we'll just fight. His mother already tells him how bad I am. I need your support.

Although divorced or separated couples often want no contact with each other, they ensure the best survival of their children by sticking together in parenting. As single parents express their doubts that their former spouses will ever cooperate, they are invited to enact the situation, first from the position of their former spouse and then from their own position. Through the role play, they learn the ways in which they themselves maintain the noncooperation. They also discover that, with a consistent commitment to cooperation, their chances of enlisting the help of their co-parent are greatly enhanced.

> She: I'm calling because your son was picked up by the police for missing school. I want you to get him to stop this. It was so embarrassing; I had to leave work to pick Carlos up.
>
> He: Well, you're finally admitting that you can't take care of him. You just wanted the support money. You take care of it.
>
> She: I don't care about the money. I'm scared. I don't mean to blame you or get you to be the bad guy. I'd really like your help to get Carlos back to school. He seems to know how to get to me.
>
> He: What do you want?
>
> She: Well, if you could come over to the school with Carlos and me to let him and the school know that we both want him in school and that we'll work together—at least in this area.
>
> He: My new wife doesn't like my talking with you. But I guess meeting at the school with Carlos is okay. I don't want him out on the streets blowing it. When do we meet?
>
> She: Thanks. How about tomorrow at 9:00?

Healthy parents allow themselves to play, even though they are grown up. They play with their children with a sense of eagerness, not of responsibility or guilt. Given time and money pressures, however, it is common for parents to lose sight of their own playful side.

Through play, parents can be nourished by their children. Play allows parents and children to step outside their roles as the enforcer and the follower of rules so that they can relate to each other in different ways. Children in the audience underline the ways they like their parents to play with them. Parents are encouraged to recollect and reinforce the ways they enjoyed playing as kids and the fun they have had with their children. They are reminded that a brief period of quality play with a child far outweighs an expensive vacation based on guilt. Few parents actually plan and take charge of playing with their children. Role plays are used to practice setting times for play.

> Child: Mom, will you play Monopoly with me?
> Mom: Not right now, honey, I'm tired.
> Child: Then, Mom, can you drive me down to Chuck E. Cheese
>   so I can play the video games?
> Mom: No. I told you I'm tired. Now stop bugging me.
> Trainer: Try setting a time and activity that you can handle.
> Mom: After I've fixed dinner and sat down for a bit, I'll have
>   some time to play with you. At 7:00. Here, you check this
>   clock (timer); when it's 7:00, you bring the Monopoly
>   game, and we'll play for an hour.

Therapists know that families must be flexible enough to change their rules as their needs change. By creating a live family sculpture with members of the audience, the life cycle of a typical family is presented. The sculpture is modified as we highlight the shifts in family structure required to address the developmental needs of family members at each stage. The sculpting is completed in 10 minutes and referred to throughout the course:

1. coupling (two people stand facing one another). This is a time of joining forces, face to face, and becoming an identifiable team. Proportionately, each one must become less the parent's child and more the partner's spouse.
2. birth of first child (couple shifts to stand side by side, enter child who stands slightly closer to mother). As a child enters this family, the couple must make room for the child and become parents. No one of the three people should regularly feel left out. Mothers typically bond first to the new child. In healthy families, the mother is sure to include the father; the father includes himself; and both adults make time to be together as a couple. At this time the parents' parents become grandparents. Parents and grandparents must negotiate a *mutually* satisfying grandparent relationship.
3. adolescence (mother steps back several steps from child, father nearer the mother and slightly closer than she to child). As families prepare to launch a child into adulthood, the parenting team usually trades responsibilities. The parent who has borne primary responsibilty for the day-by-day raising of the child, typically the mother, must become relatively less involved to make room for the child's emancipation. Concurrently, the other parent, who traditionally has been to a greater degree responsible for the family's interface with the larger world, must temporarily take on a greater responsibility for the care of the

child. This parent sanctions the child's ability to enter the adult world through increased contact with him or her.

4. empty nest (child and three grandparents leave; one grandparent sits in a chair, and parents face one another). As the demands of parenting are reduced, couples rediscover one another. Siblings reconnect to help aging parents and/or to reorganize following the death of parents.

As is the case throughout the course, the emphasis here is on the derailment of normal people by normal problems and the successful negotiation of predictably high stress times through the application of the basic tenets of healthy families. The generic components of healthy divorced, single-parent, and blended family structures are sculpted, and the transition demands identified.

1. divorce (parents stand far apart, child near one parent and waving to the other). Divorced people must develop two intact family units from what used to be one. They must develop and maintain cooperation as parents as they stop being a couple. Children need access to both parents and to all grandparents.
2. single parents (with same sex friend standing next to each parent, child stands for a few minutes next to each parent). Successful single parents have at least one close adult friend; they have a workable co-parenting arrangement; and they support their child's relationship with the former spouse.
3. blended family (two children, standing on either side of a couple holding hands; each one of the couple has a hand on the shoulder of a child; each child looks toward the other parent, who is standing nearby). Blended families must allow time for their family to form. Couples must make time to be together, which is harder when they are already parents; children must be allowed continued loyalty to their biological parent as they develop bonds with their stepparent.

At the end of this first session the content is summarized and the "rules" for participation in the course delineated:

1. The trainers will operate as consultants to families.
2. The families will bring their own life stories to the course.
3. Everyone is responsible for the success of the course.
4. Everyone gets credit for the success of the course.

The following are sample responses from the evaluations after the first session:

1.   What did you like about this session?

- Helped me feel at ease with myself because I thought I was being unfair with rules in my household.
- Liked emphasis on parents being in control—I'm sick of hearing from others how a family should be democratic, it doesn't work for me.
- In spite of the large group, it felt very personal and safe.
- It was helpful having others express like problems, helpful hearing instructors give alternative suggestions on communication during role play.
- Fun to share ideas, nice to know how we are doing as parents in comparison to others.

2.   What would you change?

- Maybe a smaller group or time afterwards to ask personal questions that you may feel shy about asking in front of everyone.
- A suggestion box.
- Make it longer—longer each evening and longer for the series, there is so much to cover, so much to learn, so much to absorb and change.
- Next time I would bring the rest of my family.

3.   What do you want to learn from this session?

- I don't know, but so far so good. Reaffirms what I believe, know and do in a world where it seems many parents have given up.
- To deal with three generations living together under tension.
- How to be more in charge and set boundaries. I get inconsistent, unsure, scared, and am often manipulated by my daughter (4) and at 4 I know things will be out of control at 16—as they were for me and my father, a single parent also.
- How to discuss sex with children and to handle sexual feelings such as where to draw the line when cuddling.

- I got to realizing that I am afraid of my own anger—don't know how to cope with it responsibly—the thought of physically constraining a teenager frightens me because of my own anger.
- How to get support from grandparents.
- To have more faith in myself as a parent.

4. What would you like other classes on?

- The unique needs of Mexican families
- Being a stepmother.
- How to live with parents-in-law.
- A special class for parents of kids who are on drugs.

Week 2: How to Survive as a Child in a Healthy Family

The rules presented in the second session are as follows:

1. Get good at something.
2. Bring something good home.
3. Follow home rules.
4. Learn about rules outside the home.

For this session, children are invited to sit with one another, away from their parents. The goal for the session is to allow children some power in their families without weakening parental authority. Children in healthy families do two things: they begin to develop themselves as individuals, and they learn how best to use their power at home. All children can become good at something, and this helps them to feel good about themselves and to get recognition from others. Children have a responsibility to contribute to the well-being of their families. By bringing home new skills, good grades, or success stories, children influence how parents feel and respond to them.

Being a child in a family is a temporary role. While in this role, children need to learn the rules of their home, neighborhood, school, and clubs. Children who live sometimes with one parent and sometimes with the other need to learn the rules of each home. By following the rules in the home, children receive more caring and make it possible to negotiate for what they want.

Ann:	I'm never allowed to go to a dance, and all my friends go.
Trainer:	What do you want?
Ann:	To go.
Trainer:	OK. One of us will play your parent. Which parent do you want to talk to first?
Ann:	I just have a mom.
Trainer:	*(pointing to the other trainer)* OK, Ginny will be your Mom. See if you can follow the rules for kids as a way to help you get what you want.
Ann:	Well, why can't I go? All the other girls are going.
Mom:	You aren't those other girls. You are 13 years old. Maybe those parents don't care, but I do.
Ann:	But Mom!
Mom:	*(angry)* Don't talk back to me! You're not ready to go to any dance.
Ann:	You're just too strict.
Trainer:	Are things going the way you want?
Ann:	Heck, no.
Trainer:	Try again, and this time let your mom know that you appreciate her concerns. Give her some examples of how you've been responsible and followed the rules.
Ann:	Mom, look, I've always gotten good grades. I let you know if I am going to be late from school. I come in on time. *(teasing playfully)* Now will you let me? Huh? Huh?
Mom:	*(softening)* You're right, you've been a good kid. I just don't want you getting hurt.
Ann:	I don't want to either! You could drive me and pick me up, and they keep us inside for the whole dance.
Mom:	Let me think about it, and I'll tell you tonight.
Trainer:	That was very nice. You have a lot better chance of getting what you want with your mom on your side. Thank you for coming up.

The trainers model the interrelatedness of people in this session. The trainers are now part of the system of parents and children. Rather than undermining the parental team and appearing to be the ally of the children, the trainers support the parental role. In contrast to the first session, which focused on the parents, the second session focuses on the children, giving the parents an opportunity to experience the trainers telling the children that

It is their responsibility to help the parents make the family healthy. As role plays unfold, the rewards children can receive for deferring to their parents' position and expressing their freedom within the limits of the house rules are made clear to children and parents alike. Children are reminded that they may not like or agree with their parents' decisions, but that families work best when the adults are in charge.

Week 3: How to Survive as a Couple in a Healthy Family

The rules to be discussed in the third session are

1. Be a couple.
2. Make room for the coupling dance.
3. Know what you want.
4. Say what you want.
5. Get what you want.

For the first time in the course, the audience is broken into small groups (that do not include partners). Their task is to talk for 20 minutes about what brought them together with their partner and what keeps them together. People without partners discuss what brought them to their single life and what keeps them in it. Afterward, the larger group reviews some of the highlights of the small group discussions.

This is a pivotal session. Most adults find it easier to express their parental concerns than to look at their life as a couple. A couple is defined as a union of two people that is formed to fill mutual needs and persists over time. Only adults are invited to this session, but they need not currently be one of a couple to attend or benefit from it. Nontraditional couples, such as two single mothers sharing a household, homosexual couples, college roommates, and "about to be" couples, should be specifically included.

Every adult needs another adult with whom he or she can share feelings, thoughts, and events. Couples go through stages. The dance of couples requires that, while they are developing their relationship, they also renegotiate other relationships, especially those with parents and children. Coupling requires time to play, talk, fight, rest, move apart, and come close. Surviving as a couple requires skills to go beyond expectations and unexamined roles until each partner knows clearly and behaviorally what he or she needs from the other, skills to say exactly what he or she wants; and skills to stick to the subject, compromise, and negotiate.

Question from   What if you know what you want and say it, and he still
the audience: doesn't pay attention?

Trainer: Will you come up here and act out what you want? We'll
help you get it.

She: Sure. *(comes to the front)* He's always too busy to spend
any time with me, even to plan things to do together. He's
got his little projects to do and the plants in the greenhouse.

Trainer: *(moving into role of husband)* Do you want something, or
can I go work on my plants?

She: I want to be with you and feel closer. We never talk anymore. All you ever do is spend time with your plants. We
don't even go anywhere.

2nd Trainer: Are you getting what you want? Sounds more like blaming.
You've held this in for a long time and have some resentment. Now, in talking to him, let him know what you want—
not just in ideas, but in action. Act with him the way you
want him to act with you. Try talking to him differently.

She: *(moving over and touching his arm)* I miss you and like it
when you can take time to play with me like we used to.

He: What's the matter with you? Stop touching me! Everything
is fine. We get along fine. Now, is that all? I have some
work to do.

She: *(tugging at his arm and then getting up to walk with him)*
I'm glad you're talking. You are really important to me, and
even a few moments talking with you is important to me. I'll
just walk out with you and then come back in here and do
my work, too.

He: *(nervous with his wife's insistence, but at the same time
liking it, jokes)* Don't go in the greenhouse with me. You
know how the plants react to you. *(everyone laughs)*

Trainer: *(to wife)* OK, stop for a moment. What have you done
differently, and is it working for you?

She: I didn't blame him or get into an argument, and we're
laughing together.

Trainer: Yes, it's not all you want, but it's better than usual, and
each time together like this makes the next time easier.

She: It was different for me, being playful with him and noticing
that, while I was *asking* for intimacy and time, I was actually getting listened to and having time with him.

The majority of this session is devoted to building negotiating skills. People are taught to get beyond the words *commitment* and *intimacy* to the actual behaviors that define these words and make them a reality. For example, instead of saying, "I want more intimacy with you," we suggest saying, "Let's go out to dinner without the children tonight." In order to make requests specific, however, people must know what they want in the first place. This session offers people a chance to say what they want and then negotiate for it in such a way that both partners "win." We also teach people to recognize when they have achieved their objective and should stop negotiating.

A typical comment from the evaluation illustrates how people begin to integrate these skills into their lives:

> This session touched on areas we (my husband and I) are going through right now. It's so much work to know what exactly it is I want from him. It sometimes takes weeding through the muck before needs are really brought up. It was helpful to talk about this, also to mention how we blame one another. It's so easy to do this.

Week 4: How to Survive as a Family during Hard Times

The rules presented in the fourth session are

1. Know when you are in hard times.
2. Face hard times together.
3. Take your time.
4. Ask for outside help when your family is stuck.

In this session, we acknowledge that all families go through hard times, such as the death of a grandparent or the loss of a job. Even seemingly positive experiences, such as the birth of a child, can produce a great deal of stress in a family. Early in the session, members of the audience are asked to comment on hard times they have faced and how they have handled them.

> Our son was picked up by the police for shoplifting. We were shocked and wondered where we went wrong. Our minister helped us to see that Bruce has to bear responsibility for his actions.

My mother is senile. It was tearing me apart to think of putting her in a nursing home. My wife got me to talk about it, then we found a way to keep her at home with help. I feel much better.

These examples illustrate to the audience that the community already has a wealth of experience and knowledge with which to confront hard times constructively.

Because healthy families face hard times as they arise, they do not face chronic internal hard times, such as alcoholism or child abuse. In families with good coping skills, *all* the family members study the situation facing them and help to solve it. Often, particularly in the case of death, families forget to include the children.

Healthy families avoid blaming one another or suffering silently. There is a steady move toward resolution, not a rush for quick and simple answers. While healthy families take their time, using their own feelings, their own thoughts, and their own internal resources, they do not hesitate to ask for outside help from extended family, friends, or professionals if the stress continues.

In this role play, a 19-year-old man is encouraged to renew contact with his father, whom he has seen only three times in the last 10 years. One trainer plays the father; the other coaches the son.

Son:	What if you can't remember anything good about your dad, and it's been over 10 years since you lived with him?
Trainer:	Come on up and talk to him.
Son:	*(to trainer)* But I want *him* to come to me, to want to talk to me.
Trainer:	Sure you do. Let him know that now, and take your time. It's been 10 years.
Son:	Dad, I want to talk to you. I was thinking that I can't remember anything we've done together, anything good, since I was a little kid. I want to be able to talk to you, have you around.
Father:	So.
Son:	I need you in my life, Dad. Not just once in a while. You know, I'm always the one who goes to visit you. I want you to visit me once in a while.
Trainer:	*(gently to son)* You're doing fine, take it slowly and don't blame.

Father: Look, Son, I don't talk much. I'm sorry. I'm not going to change. Just grow up and take care of yourself. Just leave me alone and take care of your own life.

Son: No way. I want you for my dad, and I'm going to have you.

Trainer: *(touches son's shoulder)* He's talking to you now. Ask him to help you remember things you did together when you were little.

Son: Once we went fishing, just you and me.

Father: Yeah, that was up Pinto Creek . . . trout.

This session has consistently been the most powerful one in the series. The material presented is not new; it elaborates on the principles stated in earlier sessions. In this session, however, the trainers show how the resources developed in the previous sessions can be combined to establish a base for handling hard times. This session also provides participants with an awareness of the signals or symptoms of problems and families' coping styles. Participant interest generally warms to the task of identifying problematic behavior, so guidance is required to keep a balance between diagnosing pathological states and developing prevention skills.

A momentum has developed as the course has progressed and people have learned, practiced, and changed with one another. As participants gain confidence and skill, they take bigger risks and invite coaching through complex family difficulties. The trainers continue to use the same tools they have relied on throughout the program. They use family life cycle material to maintain a focus on the normalcy of change and stress; structural family therapy concepts to shape family scenes, enactments as the vehicle for change, and the contract to teach "rules for healthy families" as the boundary of their role with the audience. Especially in this fourth session, trainers must remain clearly in their role as trainers and not succumb to the temptation to become therapists on stage.

One ever-evolving tool is the availability of the audience as teachers of one another. The trainers consciously increase their reliance on the audience to advise each other and identify patterns of health as they move toward the final session.

Week 5: How to Survive as a Family with Other Families

Rules discussed in the fifth session are

1. Use your relatives as resources.
2. Establish friendships.

3. Use relatives and friends to connect you with resources.
4. Use resources.

In the sessions leading to this final one, families have been using their own lives as input for the course content. They have been talking to other families with similar problems. Now the focus expands to include the networks within extended families and within the community—networks that serve the family. Participants are challenged to see relatives as positive resources in their families, rather than as problems or unfinished business, and to align themselves with relatives in a way that builds and maintains linkages. Once several generations of family members have been incorporated into a resource system, the next step is to use this resource system as a bridge to connect to the broader community resources.

Effective consumers approach community resources and professionals as equals. Many people feel intimidated by professionals, whether they be teachers, attorneys, social workers, physicians, or counselors. By using the principles taught in the session for couples—know, say, and get what you want—participants can overcome their timidity in using resources and in dealing with professionals.

> Trainer: Give me your example.
>
> Husband: What if outside resources don't work? We've asked our daughter to come to these sessions. We've talked to her social worker. We've paid for her therapy. She still doesn't take care of her baby or do the things she should.
>
> Trainer: Come up here with your wife, and we'll help you.
>
> Husband: Well, you better help my wife because she can't say no. Besides, our daughter is—well, she's got some emotional problems and can't take care of herself very well. She was married and now she's divorced and living with us. We help her take care of her 3-year-old daughter.
>
> Wife: (to husband) We can't just throw her out of the house, you know. She is trying. She's supposed to get a job next month, and then she'll get an apartment and move out and not need us so much.
>
> Husband: (sighs) She'll always need us.
>
> Wife: Don't be so hard on her.
>
> Trainer: Look, let's talk about you two and not your daughter. What would you like to do in handling your daughter?

	What do you two want, and how can you help each other?
Husband:	Sure, except it won't work. She'll give in. Every time we're somewhere else, she'll drop everything and help our daughter. If we're at a restaurant and our daughter calls, she goes right out and helps her.
Female Trainer:	(*to wife, teasing softly*) Really! Wow. What a MOTHER!
Male Trainer:	(*to husband*) Then you help her. You teach her how to say no. You seem to have the ability to say no, and your wife could use your help. So you be the one to answer and say no. OK?
Husband:	Sure.
Trainer:	(*telephone ringing*) Hello, Dad, I need to talk to Mom to help me with the baby.
Husband:	No, take care of it yourself. Goodbye. (*hangs up the phone, audience cheers*)
Wife:	(*laughing*) He'd never say that.
Trainer:	He said it. (*to husband*) Now your wife isn't too happy with this answer. Give her some attention.
Both:	(*crying, as he touches her and holds her*) We really love each other. We like to do things together.
Trainer:	Appreciate how nicely you two have stuck together and used each other as resources—turning to the one who can do what you both want to do.

Family systems therapists know how to enter a system, initiate change, and leave. As the course progresses, the trainers gradually deemphasize their profile as experts and rely on the audience to reinforce the training with one another. Members of the audience offer suggestions to a person stuck in a family scene, spontaneously demonstrate how they might get beyond a certain point, share how they are now in charge in an area where they had been floundering, and linger after the session, building friendships. It is hoped that family members will leave this series with a conviction, based on experience, that their family can thrive. The more they practice, the more convinced they become. Like a family, the community of families survives best when its member families stick together

At the end of this final session, we celebrate. Participants and trainers are congratulated, and certificates are given out in recognition of those who have completed the series.

CONCLUSION

The survival rate for therapists in individual practice is poor. Given a chance to have an impact on large groups of people, experience team support, and use their creativity to its full extent, most therapists experience new energy and appreciation of their skills. The highly refined skills involved in assessing and defining pathological conditions find new life in preventive models that focus on strengths. Skills for entering family systems come alive with large groups of interested parents. The drama of the therapists' work is appreciated in the theater of training and in the context of developing roles and strategies to build personal and family health.

Families set the health tone for their members. At this time, large numbers of American families are unable to provide an environment rich enough to allow for the continued development of their members. They need new tools if they are to reclaim their central role, and the field of family therapy is sufficiently sophisticated to offer those tools. This model not only translates family therapy information and methods into a form readily available to the general population, but also represents a new role for therapists, one that we have found invigorating and gratifying.

REFERENCE

Minuchin, S. *Families and family therapy.* Cambridge, MA: Harvard University Press, 1974.

10. Clinical Use of the Family Life Cycle: Some Cautionary Guidelines

Howard A. Liddle, EdD
Director, Behavioral Sciences Program
Division of Family and Community Medicine
University of California
School of Medicine

Faculty
Mental Research Institute
Palo Alto, California

George W. Saba, PhD
Director of Training
Midwest Family Resource Associates
Chicago, Illinois

THE RECENT INTRODUCTION OF THE FAMILY LIFE CYCLE PARADIGM INTO the mainstream of family therapy has been a welcome conceptual advancement. Yet, its influx into the field must be seen in a developmental context. It arrives at a time when other theories and concepts are also struggling to take hold in family therapists' collective consciousness. The epistemologic renewal, research innovations, dialogues about models of treatment, advances in ethnicity and cross-cultural sensitization, and pragmatic contributions in the areas of resistance and engagement of traditionally hard-to-reach families are but a few indications of family therapy's evolution in a more complex and sophisticated direction. Two important threads of family therapy's development have been the specification of distinct schools of thought and certain advances that are applicable across theoretical positions. The family life cycle paradigm is one of these developments; it is a template that transcends theoretical allegiance. When examined from the perspective of a particular theoretical viewpoint, however, it can assist that perspective in becoming more appropriately complex.

Although a distinctive and substantive addition, the family life cycle paradigm is still at a formative stage, both in its internal development and in its interconnection to the broader field of family therapy. Like families, concepts have their own evolutionary cycles. The earliest endeavors in the active application of the family life cycle concept to a clinician's work have probably been more helpful in a consciousness-raising sense than in a truly pragmatic way (Haley, 1974; Solomon, 1973). More recent efforts have not only elaborated the specifics of a family life cycle paradigm, but also begun to define the ways in which it has clinical relevance (Carter & McGoldrick, 1980; McGoldrick & Carter, 1982; Walsh, 1982). The concept has now evolved sufficiently to be therapeutically useful, at least in a general, orienting sense, but it must also be considered ill-formed enough to carry a risk of misuse or potential harm to therapeutic efforts. Our intent is to make explicit some of the complexities involved in clinical implementation of the family life cycle so that therapists can, in light of our current level of knowledge and concept formation, be cognizant of the realistic, developmentally understandable limitations of this model.

CONCEPT AS ICON

At various points in the development of family therapy, new trends and concepts have helped clinicians sharpen their therapeutic skills. However, enthusiasm for such discoveries and the ever-present political and personal contexts in which these developments occur has often encouraged a faddish allegiance to conceptual messiahs. Reverence for a concept tends to stall its development and thus reduce its effective utilization. The double bind, cult formation around the schools of family therapy, epistemologic issues (e.g., the aesthetics-pragmatics debate), and, most recently, ethnicity and cross-cultural sensitivity are potential cases in point. Given the possibilities, therefore, of concept reverence, overgeneralization, and (perhaps paradoxically) underutilization, the emergence of the family life cycle concept demands sober attention.

Thus, as promising, new concepts emerge in family therapy, a reductionistic temptation can emerge in many forms. The conduct of family therapy is a complex endeavor, so much so that, as new concepts appear, it is tempting to view them as clinical panaceas. The desire for simplicity and a proved therapeutic path often leads to a naive and narrow perspective, replete with utopian expectations for universally workable clinical magic. It is this tendency that must be counteracted in adapting the family life cycle concept to therapeutic work.

One device that might be useful in this regard is the visual metaphor of conceptual transparencies. The use of an overhead projector can increase the viewer's capacity to understand ever-greater degrees of conceptual complexity, as the clear plastic transparencies are placed one on top of the other. The family life cycle, ethnicity and cross-cultural factors, and the key dimensions of any therapeutic approach (e.g., premises of change, role of the therapist, conceptions about normative and dysfunctional behavior) might all be considered conceptual overlays or templates. By superimposing these and other conceptual transparencies in their mind's eye, therapists can adapt a therapeutic blueprint to guide them in each clinical situation and can increase their control over the degree of therapeutic complexity they choose to employ (Liddle, 1982b). Of course, when therapists unrealistically overload their "conceptual overhead projector" with too many templates, confusion rather than clarity of options can prevail. Furthermore, when transparencies of noncomplementary therapeutic orientations—those offering inconsistent or contrary suggestions of goals or therapeutic strategy—are superimposed, additional problems arise (Liddle, 1982a). Given these potential drawbacks, however, the transparency technique has been easily used by a variety of clinicians and found to be an effective, positive training and self-supervision device. It allows therapists to select which conceptual overlays are most essential (given their experience, therapeutic approach, treatment context, and the presenting problem and family) and to use them simultaneously. The transparencies comprise a personally constructed therapeutic lens that can expand, contract, and change in accordance with a therapist's intended focus.

THE FAMILY LIFE CYCLE AS A THERAPEUTIC GUIDE: PROMISE AND PROBLEMS

The main contributions of the family life cycle paradigm in its present degree of development seem to lie not in the explicit prescription or direction of a therapist's behavior, but in the addition of a crucial temporal dimension to understanding a family's functioning and in the extension of the focus on processes over the life span. Furthermore, the obvious emphasis on human behavior as a developmental process has discouraged a therapeutic posture focused on pathological conditions.

Yet, an appreciation of the particular number or sequence of expectable stages, or of the family processes inherent in each of these stages and transition points does not alone guide or dictate therapist behavior. Such an understanding may provide a therapeutically useful developmental frame for therapist and family, may sensitize the family to the inevitability of struggle, crisis, and difficulty in managing constant transitions; and may define problems in a way that, by implication or deduction, prescribes a therapist's interventions. As a single template or conceptual transparency, however, the family life cycle concept *is* limited in the specific therapist behavior(s) it suggests. In this way, the family life cycle is currently more a framework for understanding and assessment, and perhaps for goal setting, as well as a potential framing mechanism (putting behavior in developmental context), than a roadmap for therapeutic action.

Nevertheless, when used in conjunction with a clearly articulated approach to therapy, the family life cycle can serve as a useful and, perhaps necessary but not sufficient, conceptual overlay. An outstanding contemporary example of how the family life cycle can be applied to a therapist's work is the leaving home model of Haley (1980). In this case, Haley adapted his strategic therapy approach to one particular population—young adults and their families having difficulties in the mutual transitions required when offspring become independent. In the leaving home approach, Haley applied a set of premises about therapy and change developed in multiple contexts to a specific life cycle stage. Haley's theory of therapy and ideas about family life cycle issues at one particular phase of family development co-evolve together in a dynamic, dialectical interchange. The two domains comprise an interdependent, inseparable, interrelated whole—a context called the leaving home model—that can serve as a prototype for a therapist's quest to integrate the family life cycle concept into clinical practice.

Theoretical Issues

The family therapy movement has always contained the potential for a family chauvinism—a reductionism, at one level, no different and no less problematical than the monadic epistemology of former years. Thus, a periodic reminder of the inevitable existence and influence of extrafamilial systems on individual lives is needed. An overfocusing on the family as the only evolving unit of significance is to misuse and misinterpret the systems viewpoint.

With the family life cycle approach, the family must be seen as a system that has a life cycle (predictable stages) of its own; however, the family life cycle schema must incorporate an understanding of the individual developmental stages of its members and, perhaps more importantly, an understanding of the relationships, interconnections, and mutual influence of these individual life cycles on one another. Use of the family life cycle does not make it necessary to ignore the relevance of individual life stages, just as a family therapy view does not preclude definition of individuals as systems (the individual is both whole and part, to paraphrase Koestler). Thus, future models of the family life cycle must take into account the co-evolution of life stages, i.e., one in relation to the other, as well as the co-evolution of the family life cycle in relation to its broader macrosystemic subsystems. In discussing the interrelationship between the level of social structures and the level of "cultural guiding images," Markley (1976) suggested just such a co-evolutionary relationship, in which each level alternately pulls and is pulled by the other.

Along these lines, Terkelsen's (1980) paper, "Toward a Theory of the Family Life Cycle," seems to be a step in the needed direction. He discussed the developmental interaction effects within the family life cycle, i.e., the notion that the "developmental particulars of each family member are shaped by, and in turn shape, the particulars of each other member's development. Each member's growth is a stimulus in present time for growth in each other member" (p. 42). This kind of model building can help to keep the family life cycle paradigm away from the static, non-process-focused diagnostic schemas historically used in mental health. In the main, however, models accounting for the complex, interconnecting nature of multiperson, multicontext, and multigenerational effects from a developmental perspective are still to be constructed.

Theory of Change

For a family life cycle paradigm to be useful to therapists, it must address the notion of the nature of change at more than a macroscopic level. The temptation to speak vaguely about transitions and evolution from one stage to another is great and must be avoided. Thus far, processes that happen within expectable stages, as well as dysfunctional patterns surrounding "failed" transitions, have been identified, but few links have been made between a theory of human developmental change and clinical change.

Terkelsen (1980) effectively applied systemic principles of interaction to human development:

> When one member attains a new level of individual maturation, alterations in family unit structure follow. Those alterations are much more extensive than is generally realized. In point of fact, even very small, incremental developments can produce surprisingly widespread perturbations in family structure. Trace what happens when a child in an imaginary family of five learns to dress herself:
>
>> The elements of structure attached to the old need (mother dresses child, and simultaneously engages in reciprocal nurturing by giving attention, physical contact, verbal repartee) drop away. Child and parent seek out new behavioral sequences that allow the child to dress herself, and create an alternative format for reciprocal nurturing. For example: child enters kitchen, announces, "Mommy, I dress myself!" Mother praises her, helps her into a chair, brings her food, and straightens her dress.
>
> However, these alterations also trigger *trials of new behavior in other family members*, as adaptations to the new element of structure. Inevitably, conflict emerges between elements of structure that were previously well-integrated, but are now dyssynchronous. For example:
>
>> Instead of dressing her child, mother now goes directly to the kitchen, and has more time to attend to her husband and two boys. Husband gets fed faster, but

now finds himself criticized for reading at breakfast. The boys have more time for verbal repartee with mother, but simultaneously have acquired an increase in maternal supervision of their play. Father, in turn, may object to mother's supervision, initiating a discordant interaction between husband and wife. And so on. (pp. 35-36)

Terkelsen came closer to the needed bridge between clinical and life cycle formulations of change in his description of the three phases of developmental change:

1. an insertion stage, in which new needs are recognized and validated, and new behavioral trials are begun
2. a destabilization phase, in which new sequences that can clash with existing patterns are added
3. a resolution stage, in which a compromise structure gradually takes hold and relative stability increases

Hoffman (1981, 1982) has presented another model of change in families that can be explored isomorphically at the levels of clinical change and family development. In formulating her model of discontinuous change, Hoffman has adapted the ideas of physicists Prigogine and Platt, as well as cybernetician Ashby. This perspective favors what evolutionists call a punctuational (Gould, 1982; Stanley, 1981) view of change. In Hoffman's (1981) words, families "do not change in a smooth, unbroken line but in discontinuous leaps" (p. 158). Hoffman argued against any gradualist, continuous notions of change, asserting that families, like other complex living systems, change by means of sudden transformations with the appearance of more functionally organized behavior previously nonexistent in the system.

The natural history of a leap or transformation is usually as follows. First, the patterns that have kept the system in a steady state relative to its environment begin to work badly. New conditions arise for which these patterns were not designed. Ad hoc solutions are tried and sometimes work, but usually have to be abandoned. Irritation grows over small but persisting difficulties. The accumulation of dissonance usually forces the entire system over an edge, into a state of crisis, as the homeostatic tendency brings on ever-intensifying corrective sweeps that get out of control. The end point of what cybernetic engineers call a "runaway" is either that the system breaks down, creates a new way to monitor the same homeostasis, or else may spontaneously take a leap to a new integration that will deal better with the changed field. (Hoffman, 1980, p. 56; 1981, p. 160)

Another dimension is the factor of time, or the definition of when change can be said to occur. A discontinuous-only description creates the illusion of specificity (Whitehead's fallacy of misplaced concreteness) regarding the timing of change. How is it possible to be so sure that change has occurred precisely at the (apparent) leap of transformation? Such leaps are compelling, dramatic descriptors, but they are weak on explanatory substance. Some physicists were equally convinced of the particle aspects of subatomic matter until their colleagues saw the identical reality in a different way—as a wave or process. A discontinuous interpretation of change encourages snapshot-like slices of what, from other perspectives, would be seen as process versions of reality. The concept of time is therefore crucial here from the point of view of considering when the assessment (and punctuation) of change occurs. A discontinuous paradigm shines the spotlight of change evaluation only onto noticeable changes. Outside this ring of illumination, however, are less clearly discernible aspects of the change in question. In these shadows may lurk the precursors and consequences of transformation, perhaps vital components of an advanced understanding of the process and context of human change.

Finally, there is the cybernetic, on-off, all-or-nothing, change or no-change perspective that the discontinuous view encourages. From this vantage point, concepts such as trial-and-error learning, successive approximations, the readiness or availability of a context to change (a potentially lineal, yet underexplored notion from a systems view), and a system's apparently natural tendencies to resist change unfortunately have little room for development.

Just as beginning therapists often have difficulties focusing on a single theme, content area, or subsystem (perhaps fearing they will miss something crucial) and oscillate too rapidly between these potential areas of intervention, family members can demonstrate the same kind of oscillation between stages in the life cycle.[1] For example, a single parent might be treated by her own mother like an inept child in need of help rather than like the struggling, yet able mother she is striving to be. In this case, the mother might oscillate between the generational pulls of her mother, who tempts her with promises of assistance in the struggles of a single parent, and her daughter, who challenges her with a complex and evolving set of demands. In this example, the difficulty with the cybernetically related, all-or-nothing, on-off analogy of discontinuous change can be readily seen. Determining which stage of the family life cycle the family members are "in" is similar to the static reductionism of the diagnostician searching for the correct classification. This kind of activity produces an illusion of understanding about the human condition, and suggests that change is a one-step affair (at point A it has not happened, at point B it has). From this perspective, the useful and appropriately sophisticated notion of stages (of therapy, of change) (Haley, 1976, 1980) is, unfortunately, ignored.

Hoffman's clearly articulated views on discontinuous change as it applies to the family life cycle raise several substantive, yet debatable, issues. First, it must be recognized that the application of concepts and metaphors from other fields to family therapy has both strong benefits and significant limitations. The ability to remain an open system and to keep cognizant of theoretical and pragmatic advances in other domains of knowledge should be a high priority for family therapists, who must be specialists in the art of understanding interrelatedness. At the same time, the wholesale adoption of constructs from other contexts is a potentially misleading and conceptually muddled endeavor. It can amount to the epitome of ecology-chopping—the cardinal sin of systems thinkers. It inexplicably ignores the principle of contextual relativity—the premise that what may be a helpful truth in one world may be a less than helpful, or even handicapping falsehood in another.

Second, in a stance that construes discontinuous transformation as the only form of change, other, equally plausible explanations of the same interactional phenomena might be omitted. To see only discontinuous change could be regarded as a problem of vantage point or punctuation. In this case, the focus is on a certain kind of change (that which is perceptible) at a certain point in time (after the perceptible change has occurred). Smaller transformations are impervious to the vantage point of the observer, however, and perhaps to the instrument of vision (lens, framework) as well. Indeed, if discontinuous leaps are considered the only way in which true change occurs, nondiscontinuous "leaps" (perhaps "steps") would be outside the available reality and would represent a different, but not necessarily competing world view. Bateson (1979) struggled with this difficulty of perception and interpretation:

> All receipt of information is necessarily the receipt of news of difference and all perception of difference is limited by threshold.

Differences that are too slowly presented are not perceivable.
They are not food for perception. (p. 29)

Thus, from this vantage point, it seems wisest to consider a number of interlocking factors in addressing the process of developmental and clinical change.

Stages and Processes

Debate over the definitive number of life cycle stages or preoccupation with the phenomenologic processes within each stage represent well-intentioned effort in a less than productive direction. It seems mandatory, therefore, to underscore the essence of the family life cycle—the dynamic interplay of transition and stability within and between subsystems. Any family life cycle paradigm must include clear statements about precisely how change (transitions) occurs through the life cycle; it must define whose change is being discussed (change from whose perspective) and what kind of change is being considered. Finally, of course, change must be described in a contextual manner; this perspective must account for the multiple influences of several contexts, and levels of a single context, in the change process.

Continued use of the concept of a family being "stuck" in a given stage seems unwarranted. Not only does the concept imply a static or frozen quality to life, but also it is descriptively imprecise and vague. The concrete image provoked by the term *stuck* is helpful only to describe development's retardation in a broad, generic way. In addition, stuckness implies that, without help, the family will continue in its problematic way. In fact, fortuitous life events, as well as what therapists consider "deviant" behavior, repeatedly spark and influence change. Families, as Bateson (1979) might say, "feed on the random" continuously in solving their own problems and in finding ways to utilize internal resources in the successful negotiation of life's transitions.

A more productive way in which to view difficulty in transitions is to look for specific examples of behavioral oscillation within and between the stages of the life cycle. Such a view of the process of developmental change seems to be a more realistic approach to the natural difficulty, ambivalence (not necessarily an intrapsychic concept), and struggle of movement through life.

The question might be asked—when is a family not in a life stage transition? Such a focus might help to take the unneeded attention away from the critical period theory. Certainly some periods seem more critical than others; yet, there is often a heightened sense of pseudocertainty about determining exactly when a family is in crisis about the needed change(s).

The visual images provoked by the family life cycle framework (as by any framework) can be interpreted too literally. With any metaphor of movement from one stage to another, there is a tendency to emphasize the destination rather than the journey. The "progress" of transition can suggest that family members are leaving something (a condition or state) that is dysfunctional and moving "into" a stage that will necessarily be more healthy. Life cycle stages, furthermore, can be seen as discrete, completely definable, and predictable entities rather than as societally, culturally, and familially relative constructions that loosely house fluid and, in many ways highly *un*predictable interactional realities. Additionally, the journey between these arbitrarily punctuated stages need not be completely negative and crisis-filled. New aspects of one's self or others that might be pleasant and rewarding surprises may be discovered during these times of family life.

Family Life Cycle and Issues of Normality

Therapists' utilization of the family life cycle is necessarily linked to their conceptions of what constitutes healthy or normal behavior, i.e., what behaviors are expected or needed. It is inevitable that therapists' own system of premises about people in general, families, and therapy will affect their judgments about dysfunctional and healthy behaviors. As therapists, they naturally tend to see and establish, confirm, and reaffirm their beliefs about families in relation to a clinical (in-treatment) sample. Therapists are not in the position of the family practice physician, for example, who sees individuals and families at checkup points, as well as during problem times.[2] Thus, family therapists' realities about what constitutes family life is, in part, constructed by the range of families that seek treatment from them. Similarly, most do not have the vantage point of those family researchers involved in the study of healthy, well functioning families. Thus, the means by which values and content are infused into therapists' personal frameworks of therapy should be of concern for family therapy trainers.

The Many Definitions of the Family Life Cycle

It could be said that the family life cycle applies (in varying degrees) to all schools of family therapy. Yet, the importance and meaning attached to the family life cycle from these frames of reference is quite variable. Thus, the importance of this construct, even its definition, must be clarified within each theoretical perspective. In the case of diagnosis and assessment, for example (Liddle, 1982c), the same construct will yield different interpretations across models. Walsh (1982) provides the kind of cross-perspective analysis in the area of normative family processes that will be helpful in the family life cycle area.

Reiss (1981) defined the idiosyncratic nature of families' world views or, as he called them, family paradigms. The family's own views and interpretations of its own family life cycle may have to be taken into account in the clinical application of the family life cycle concepts. Reiss avoided the narrow, overly predictive focus of other models, and his emphasis on how the family's own constructions of reality affect its actions perhaps provides a bilateral link missing in family life cycle theory. Therapists may have a tendency to apply their assumptions about family life cycle theory as if the family's view of itself was irrelevant! In this way, the reciprocal quality of family life cycle assessment, i.e., the ever-present interaction between a therapist's respect for a family's own idiosyncratic ways of developing and those prescriptive, value-laden templates the therapist inevitably carries into the therapeutic situation, can, unfortunately, be omitted.[3]

CONCLUSIONS

Our intent in this article has been, in essence, to contextualize the family life cycle paradigm. We have presented several aspects of any family life cycle model that need to be considered for clinicians wishing to apply the family life cycle in their work. The family life cycle does have therapeutic utility, but more sophisticated conceptualization about its definition and fit within the context of other complementary clinical frameworks is warranted and necessary.

Individuals interact with, influence, and are influenced by a variety of social systems—they hold multiple context memberships. Thus we must guard against an overly narrow interpretation of systems thinking, or in this case systems evolution in the form of the family life cycle, as the primary determinants ("causes") of human behavior. Jantsch's (1975, 1980) model of the co-evolution of macroworlds and microworlds has relevance here. Models of human development would, along these lines, describe the co-evolution of human behavior at the interdependent and interacting macrosystem and microsystem levels.

Jantsch's (1980) recommendation for a pluralism of concepts, an ecology of models can similarly be useful in the world of therapy. Family therapists, as most other psychotherapists, tend to construe human behavior only through a sociocultural lens. Jantsch considered true systems thinking much more at the level of interplay; among the social, physical, and spiritual spheres of existence.

Closer to home, the exciting work of Riegel (1975, 1976) in evolving a dialectical theory of development has tremendous implications for family therapists. Riegel emphasized the interplay of four dimensions of development: (1) inner-biological, (2) individual-psychological, (3) cultural-sociological, and (4) outer-physical. For Riegel, human development is firmly based on the interdependent, mutually influencing interactions among these four dimensions of changing events, and it aims at synchronizing progressions along these different dimensions. Riegel's conviction that "development should neither be conceived of as lying in the individual nor in the social group alone but is constituted by the dialectical interactions between both" (1975, p. 54), leads family life cycle model constructors and clinicians in a potentially useful direction. His writing models a capacity to construe development in an appropriately complex, multilayered manner.

Datan (1977) provided another fine example of dialectical thinking applied to human development. Datan's comments on a dialectical model of parent-child interaction in which the needs of each generation affect the other and discussion of the consequences generated when the needs and interests of the parent and child clash and coincide are useful in efforts to build a family life cycle model in which development can be described as mutually regulating.

Thus, the manner in which we understand the family life cycle, to paraphrase Koestler (1978) once more, as both a *whole* (a comprehensive, consistent explanatory framework) and as a *part* (*one* of the "conceptual overlays" useful in a therapist's work), will be a revealing proving ground for the same kind of activity with other newly emerging, important concepts and trends in our field (e.g., epistemologic matters and cross cultural and ethnicity perspectives). Further, just as the family life cycle presents the inevitability of the family's evolution, the family life cycle as a paradigm is itself subject to evolution (refinement and change). Therapists' beliefs about change need to be strictly tied to and developed concurrently with developing family life cycle theory. The discontinuous only view of change seems inadequate to account for the complexity and probable variety of change in human families. Jantsch's (1980) discussion of the reductionistic debate between "*quantum jumps*" (discontinuous change) and a "*gliding*" *evolution* ("Change . . . occurs in a multitude of simultaneous processes. . . . The reality of the human world becomes dissolved into many realities,"

p. 256) can be most helpful in clarifying this polemic in the family therapy field.[4]

In a related vein, we must both continue to strive for new ideas and models from other fields, yet realize their sometimes limited applicability and generalizability in their new context. Along these lines, Gould's (1980) assertion that a discontinuous, "punctuational view may prove to map tempos of *biological and geologic change* more accurately and more often than any of its competitors" (p. 185) should remind us about the dangers of model-transfer from one domain (e.g., biologic to social) to another.

Defining the family life cycle as a part of an overarching model of therapy seems to be the key to developing a realistic expectational set of its possibilities and limitations. Some approaches to psychotherapy and family therapy make little or no use of the family life cycle framework, except perhaps as a framing device for the family or therapist. One mode of inquiry in further concept development would be an examination of the family life cycle concept within each theoretical viewpoint, with an emphasis on how it is or is not used as an explanatory principle and a guide to therapeutic action. Unless the family life cycle can be clearly linked to the theories of change within any approach to therapy, it runs the risk of becoming more a framework for understanding than a blueprint for change.

As the many clinical implications of the family life cycle are explored, creative possibilities for its use will emerge. For instance, a termination assessment/intervention might be used to review a family's therapeutic progress and predict and plan for difficulties around future transitions. Thus, the family life cycle concept might have value as a therapeutic tool in sealing and generalizing changes achieved in therapy.

In the conceptual overlay metaphor, in which concept transparency is superimposed upon concept transparency, when is enough, enough? In this sense, how many and in what combination can transparencies be superimposed and still give the therapist a workable, realistic therapeutic roadmap? Furthermore, the least number and kind of conceptual keys necessary for a therapist's work are not known. Indeed, the number and kind of keys are likely to vary according to the issues in question.

As the field of family therapy becomes increasingly complex, we are led to believe that each new theme (family life cycle, cross-cultural/ethnicity, epistemology) must be incorporated into our therapeutic frameworks. Some will ask, to what degree is this increased complexity necessary to improve therapeutic effectiveness, and to what degree is this increased complexity an exercise in faddish complicity or an acquiescence to aesthetic preference? Certainly, the cluster of themes recently introduced into the field makes intuitive, perhaps even moral or ethical sense; however, those who believe in these content domains must go beyond the hyperbole and rhetoric, past the polemical and politicized nature of much of the introduction of these themes into the field. If a case is to be made for the increased complexity, preferably in terms of greater effectiveness, it must be made clearly. The family life cycle concept represents as likely and necessary an arena as any for this activity to begin. As Jantsch has pointed out, evolution is not a unilateral process, we daily participate in the design and organization of our universe.[5] The *chance* (random element) and *necessity* (purposeful, planned) of evolution, from this new view, are no longer seen as competing theories. They form a complementary, unified, dynamic whole.

NOTES

1. The idea of oscillation of family members between life cycle stages has been developed by Douglas Breunlin, a contributor in the present volume.

2. There are interesting implications regarding the very role of a family therapist here. As family medicine and family therapy begin to influence each other as subsystems, the "clinical" focus (therapists only intervene in "error-activated" systems) of family therapists might be challenged. That is, to what degree are aspects of the family practitioner's role applicable to a family therapist?

3. Reiss's (1981) research should also remind us that, as we have said, a single, universal overlay of the family life cycle will be handicapping to a therapist's needed flexibility. For instance, even if we understand the cultural/ethnic variations of the family life cycle, there will be idiosyncratic formulations and *heterogeneity* within cultures and ethnic groups.

4. Gould's essay, "The episodic nature of evolutionary change" also has relevance in this regard. For Gould (1980) "I emphatically do not assert the general 'truth' of this philosophy of punctuational change. Any attempt to support the exclusive validity of such a grandiose notion would border on the nonsensical. (I often fly over the folded Appalachians and marvel at the striking parallel ridges left standing by gradual erosion of the softer rocks surrounding them.) I make a simple plea for pluralism in guiding philosophies, and for the recognition that such philosophies, however hidden and unarticulated, constrain all our thought" (p. 185).

5. Similarly, "the psychology of chance encounters and life paths" (Bandura, 1982) extends life cycle models to yet another potential level of analysis: "A comprehensive developmental theory must . . . specify factors that set and alter particular life courses if it is to provide an adequate explanation of human behavior" (p. 747). Bandura's systemic ideas about how people *select and create* their own contexts of living, along with his discussion of the role of fortuitous events in shaping our lives nicely counters the developmental determinism this chapter has argued against.

REFERENCES

Bandura, A. The psychology of chance encounters and life paths. *American Psychologist*, 1982, *37*, 747-755.

Bateson, G. *Mind and nature*. New York: Dutton, 1979.

Carter, B., & McGoldrick, M. (Eds.). *The family life cycle*. New York: Gardner, 1980.

Datan, N. The narcissism of the life cycle. *Human Development*, 1977, *20*, 191-195.

Gould, S.J. *The panda's thumb*. New York: Norton, 1980.

Haley, J. *Problem-solving therapy*. San Francisco: Jossey-Bass, 1976.

Haley, J. *Leaving home*. New York: McGraw-Hill, 1980.

Hoffman, L. The family life cycle and discontinuous change. In B. Carter & M. McGoldrick (Eds.), *The family life cycle*. New York: Gardner, 1980.

Hoffman, L. *Foundations of family therapy*. New York: Basic Books, 1981.

Jantsch, E. *Design for evolution*. New York: Braziller, 1975.

Jantsch, E. *The self-organizing universe*. Elmsford, NY: Pergamon Press, 1980.

Koestler, A. *Janus: A summing up*. New York: Random House, 1978.

Liddle, H.A. On the problem of eclecticism: A call for epistemologic clarification and human-scale theories. *Family Process*, 1982, *21*, 243-250. (a)

Liddle, H.A. Using mental imagery to create therapeutic and supervisory realities. In A. Gurman (Ed.), *Questions and answers in the practice of family therapy* (Vol. II). New York: Brunner/Mazel, 1982. (b)

Liddle, H.A. Diagnosis and assessment in family therapy: A comparative analysis of six schools of thought. In B. Keeney (Ed.), *Diagnosis and assessment in family therapy*. Rockville, MD: Aspen Systems Corporation, 1982. (c)

Markley, O. Human consciousness in transformation. In E. Jantsch & C. Waddington (Eds.), *Evolution and consciousness*. Reading, MA: Addison-Wesley, 1976.

McGoldrick, M., & Carter, B. The family life cycle. In F. Walsh (Ed.), *Normal family processes*. New York: Guilford, 1982.

Reiss, D. *The family's construction of reality*. Cambridge, MA: Harvard University Press, 1981.

Riegel, K. Toward a dialectical theory of development. *Human Development*, 1975, *18*, 50-64.

Riegel, K. The dialectics of human development. *American Psychologist*, 1976, *19*, 689-700

Solomon, M. A developmental conceptual premise for family therapy. Family Process, 1973, *12*, 179-188.

Stanley, S. *The new evolutionary timetable*. New York: Basic Books, 1981.

Terkelsen, K. Toward a theory of the family life cycle. In B. Carter & M. McGoldrick (Eds.), *The family life cycle*. New York: Gardner, 1980.

Walsh, F. (Ed.). *Normal family processes*. New York: Guilford, 1982.